CGP

It's Another Ace Book from CGP

This book is for 12-14 year olds.

First we stick in all the _really important stuff_
you need to do well in the Key Stage Three Shakespeare Paper.

Then we have a really good stab at making it funny —
so you'll _actually use it_.

Simple as that.

CGP are just the best

The central aim of Coordination Group Publications is to produce
top quality books that are carefully written, immaculately
presented and marvellously funny — whilst always making sure
they exactly cover the National Curriculum for each subject.

And then we supply them to as many people as we possibly
can, as _cheaply_ as we possibly can.

Buy our books — they're ace

Contents

SECTION ONE — THE BASIC STUFF

Why People Hate Shakespeare 1
What Happens In The Play 2
What You've Got to Do 4
Picking Your Task 5
Reading the Bit from The Play 6
Working Out the Task 7
4 Things You Need to be Able to Do 8
Writing Well & Giving Examples 10
Revision Summary 11

SECTION TWO — UNDERSTANDING THE PLAY

Why the Play Seems Weird 12
Tricky Play Stuff 13
Tricky Play Words 14
The Setting of the Play 15
Honour 16
Family & Marriage 18
Why Life is Hard for Juliet 19
Religion 20
Revision Summary 21

SECTION THREE — READING THE LANGUAGE

Why the Language is Hard 22
Poetry In The Play 23
How To Read The Poetry 24
Different Kinds Of Poetry 26
Old Words 27
Images In The Play 28
Common Images 29
More Common Images 30
Puns & Jokes 31
Revision Summary 32

SECTION FOUR — THE MAIN CHARACTERS

Who's Who in the Play 33
Romeo 34
Juliet 35
Mercutio 36
Tybalt & Benvolio 37
Lord & Lady Montague 38
Lord & Lady Capulet 39
Nurse 40
Friar Lawrence 41
Paris, Prince & Others 42
Revision Summary 43

SECTION FIVE — UNDERSTANDING THE STORY

What Happens in Act One 44
What Happens In Act Two 47
What Happens in Act Three 50
What Happens in Act Four 53
What Happens in Act Five 55
Revision Summary 58

SECTION SIX — WRITING ABOUT CHARACTERS

Writing About Characters 59
Follow the Method 60
Finding Your Answer 61
Planning Your Answer 63
Starting Your Answer 64
Writing the Answer 65
Ending Your Answer 67
Revision Summary 68

SECTION SEVEN — WRITING AS A CHARACTER

Writing As A Character 69
Get To Grips With The Task 70
Read The Scene 71
Make Some Notes 72
Make More Notes 73
Putting Your Answer In Order 74
Answering The Question 75
Finishing It All Off 77
Revision Summary 78

SECTION EIGHT — WRITING ABOUT THE MOOD

Understanding Mood Tasks 79
Looking At The Scene 80
Reading In Detail 81
Planning Your Answer 83
Following Your Plan 84
Writing A Clear Answer 85
Using The Whole Play 86
Proving Your Points 87
Finishing Your Answer 88
Revision Summary 89

SECTION NINE — THE MOST IMPORTANT SCENES

Act 1, Scene 5 — Romeo and Juliet Meet.. 90
Act 2, Scene 2 — That Slushy Balcony Scene 92
Act 3, Scene 1 — Mercutio and Tybalt get Killed 95
Act 3, Scene 2 — Juliet isn't Happy 98
Act 3, Scene 5 — Juliet's Got to Marry Paris 100
Act 4, Scenes 1-4 — Friar Lawrence's Plan Takes Shape 103

Index 107

Published by Coordination Group Publications Ltd.

Contributors:
Angela Billington   BA (Hons), MPhil
Simon Cook   BA (Hons)
Taissa Csáky   BA (Hons)
Chris Dennett   BSc (Hons)
Dominic Hall   BSc (Hons)
Gemma Hallam   BA (Hons)
Katherine Stewart   BA (Hons)
James Paul Wallis   BEng (Hons)
Tim Wakeling   BA (Hons), GIMA
Andrew Wright   BA (Hons)

and:
Simon Little   BA (Hons)
Glenn Rogers   BSc (Hons)
Laura Schibrowski   BSc (Hons)
Claire Thompson   BSc

ISBN   1-84146-147-4

But soft, what website through yonder windows breaks: www.cgpbooks.co.uk

Jolly bits of clipart from CorelDRAW

Printed by Elanders Hindson, Newcastle upon Tyne.

0200

Why People Hate Shakespeare

You've got to write about *Romeo and Juliet* for your SAT — whether you like it or not.
It <u>doesn't matter</u> if you think it's <u>boring</u> or <u>weird</u> — just remember, it's <u>not</u> impossible.

Shakespeare <u>is</u> Dead Boring — No

Yawn...

Romeo and Juliet isn't as boring as you think. It has arguments,
fights, a love story, marriage, the betrayal of a friend, death, sex, secret plans,
fake deaths, and the main characters killing themselves for love. Phew.
There's even a film of it starring Leonardo Di Caprio and Claire Danes.

All the <u>Characters</u> have <u>Stupid Names</u>

1) Some of the characters have <u>odd-sounding</u> names, like <u>Mercutio</u>,
   <u>Tybalt</u> and <u>Benvolio</u>. That's just because they're <u>Italian</u>.

2) The play's set in <u>Verona</u> — a city in the North of <u>Italy</u>. Shakespeare
   probably <u>never</u> went there, but he <u>based</u> his play on an <u>old Italian story</u>.

Verona

   3) Lots of the things in the play are a bit <u>strange</u> to us. <u>Don't</u>
   let them <u>put you off</u>. It's only because the play is set in a
   <u>different place</u> with <u>different laws</u> and <u>customs</u>.

   4) Make sure you <u>learn</u> about the <u>main differences</u>
      between then and now — see Section Two. You have
      to <u>understand</u> the play to <u>do well</u> in your SAT.

You <u>Can't</u> Understand What Anyone's <u>Saying</u>

(1) The play's written in the <u>sort of English</u> people spoke <u>at the time</u> it was written.
     Shakespeare was a writer and poet who lived between <u>1564</u> and <u>1616</u>. He wrote
     Romeo and Juliet around <u>1595</u>. English has really <u>changed</u> since then.

(2) A lot of the play is written in <u>poetry</u>. All the <u>main</u> characters <u>speak</u> in poetry
     — that makes their speeches <u>tricky</u> to understand. They use lots of <u>weird</u>
     <u>words</u>, and their <u>sentences</u> often sound <u>jumbled up</u>.

Queen Mab hath been with you.
She is the fairies' midwife.

Eh?

> <u>Don't give up</u> right away — you just need to <u>practise</u> reading it.
> The <u>more</u> you <u>read</u> the play, the <u>easier</u> it'll get to <u>understand</u>.

Time for a break — it must be play-time...

<u>Understanding</u> the play — that's the hardest part. Just keep in mind that the <u>more</u> you read the
play, the <u>easier</u> it'll get to understand. And that means you'll do much <u>better</u> in your SAT. It's up
to you — <u>stick at it</u> and get <u>good marks</u>, or give up and do badly. It really is <u>your choice</u>.

What Happens In The Play

If you want to get <u>decent marks</u> in your Paper 2, you've got to <u>know</u> the play well. You can start by learning this summary of <u>what happens</u> in the play. Get it <u>clear in your head</u> right now.

Get the Main Events of the Play Clear in Your Head

1) The two chief families in Verona are the Montagues and the Capulets. They are enemies. A fight breaks out between some servants of the families in the street.

If I've told you once, I've told you a thousand times: NO FIGHTING

2) The ruler of Verona, the Prince, arrives and stops the fight. He tells Lord Montague and Lord Capulet, the heads of the two families, that from now on, anyone who disturbs the peace by fighting in the street will be executed.

3) Romeo, son of Montague, is in love with Capulet's niece, Rosaline. Capulet wants his daughter Juliet to marry Paris, a rich nobleman, and has a party so they can meet.

Guess who?

4) Romeo goes to the party in disguise, hoping to see Rosaline. He sees and falls in love with Juliet instead. They talk and she falls in love with him.

<u>All</u> of this stuff happens in <u>Act 1</u> of the play. An act is just a <u>section</u> of the play.

There are 5 acts in a Shakespeare play.

Act Two is Where Romeo and Juliet Get Married

5) After the feast, Romeo sneaks back to her house, and overhears her talking from the balcony of her room. She says she loves him. He speaks to her and promises that he loves her too. They agree to a secret marriage.

6) Juliet's Nurse takes messages between them and they arrange a secret wedding. They are also helped by a priest called Friar Lawrence, and they are married the next day.

Juliet wants Rome-o — but she'll always have Paris...

Knowing <u>what happens</u> in the play will help you to <u>understand</u> the bits you have to read. <u>Learn</u> these pages — well enough that you can scribble down a summary of the play <u>from memory</u>.

What Happens in the Play

This is where the action <u>really</u> gets going — make sure you learn <u>what happens</u> and <u>when</u>.

Act Three is Where Everything Starts Going Wrong

7) Tybalt, Juliet's cousin, is angry because Romeo went to the Capulet party. Mercutio, Romeo's friend, meets him, and they quarrel. Romeo arrives and tries to calm Tybalt down, but Tybalt and Mercutio fight and Mercutio is killed.

8) In rage, Romeo kills Tybalt, and runs away, realising what he's done. The Prince arrives with Montague and Capulet to find out what has happened. He banishes Romeo from Verona.

<u>Banished</u> means <u>sent away</u> — if Romeo returned to Verona, he would be executed.

9) Next day, after spending the night with Juliet, Romeo leaves for Mantua. The Friar promises to help reveal the secret of the marriage at a better moment.

10) Meanwhile, Capulet decides Juliet should marry Paris right away. He doesn't know she's married Romeo in secret. Juliet refuses but Capulet says he'll force her or throw her out on the streets.

In Act Four Juliet Fakes Her Own Death

11) Juliet goes to the Friar, who tells her to agree to the marriage, but gives her a potion to take the night before the wedding which will make her appear dead for 42 hours. He will tell Romeo to rescue her from the graveyard and take her to Mantua. Juliet fakes her own death and is placed in the family vault.

The <u>vault</u> is a sort of temple building, where <u>everyone</u> in the family is buried.

In Act Five Romeo and Juliet Die

12) Romeo doesn't get the Friar's message, and hears that Juliet is dead. He decides to go to her grave and kill himself. He buys poison. Outside the vault he meets Paris, who tries to arrest him for returning to Verona. They fight, and Paris is killed. Romeo breaks into the vault.

13) Romeo kisses Juliet, who is still unconscious, and drinks the poison and dies. Juliet wakes up and finds Romeo dead beside her. She realises what has happened, stabs herself and dies. The story is explained by the Friar and Paris's Page. Montague and Capulet are faced with the terrible result of their fighting.

The play in three words — stab and sniff...

Wow, that's a lot of action... Learning these <u>two pages</u> really will <u>help</u> you, so give it a try.

What You've Got to Do

The whole play sounds pretty long and complicated — but don't worry about that.
All you've got to do in your SAT is read one short bit from the play and do one task based on it.

You've Got to Do One Task in Your SAT

Your SAT paper will have six tasks about Shakespeare plays. Only two of them will be about *Romeo and Juliet*, so just ignore the rest. The tasks you're given are questions that ask you to write something about part of the play. They also give you loads of hints to help you with your answer.

The Narwhal only has one task... er, tusk.

Each Task has a Bit of the Play that Goes with It

1) Each task is about a particular bit of the play, and it'll tell you exactly which bit:

Act 1 Scene 1   or   Act 3 Scene 5, line 37 to the end of the scene

2) As well as the question paper, you'll get a booklet with all the different bits of the plays. Find the bits from *Romeo and Juliet*. You don't need to even look at any of the other plays.

Make Sure You Read Both Tasks Before You Choose

There are lots of different kinds of task you could be asked to do. Don't jump in with the first one you read. Look through both of them carefully before you make your mind up.

This tells you which play the task is about... **Romeo and Juliet**

Act 3 Scene 1 ...And this tells you which bit of the play.

This sets the scene — it's here to tell you what's happening in this part of the play.

TASK 1

In this scene both Mercutio and Tybalt want to start a fight.

What similarities and differences are there between Mercutio and Tybalt and who do you think is most to blame for their deaths?

Before you begin to write you should think about:

Here's the actual task — you've got to answer this question.

This tip had better be worth it...

You'll also get a sentence like this, followed by some handy tips for answering the question. They're there to help you — so make sure you use them.

Picking Your Task

It all looks a bit confusing at first. The main thing to remember is that you must read <u>both</u> tasks <u>before</u> you can decide which one you're going to answer.

There are <u>Lots</u> of <u>Different Kinds</u> of Task

① Some tasks ask you to write as if <u>you're</u> one of the <u>characters</u> from the play.

> Act 2 Scene 4, line 82 to the end of Scene 5
>
> ### TASK 2
>
> In these scenes, the Nurse is the messenger between Romeo and Juliet.
>
> **Imagine you are the Nurse. Write about your thoughts and feelings as you look back on the day's events.**

You've got to <u>pretend</u> to be the Nurse, and think about what <u>she</u> would <u>think</u> and <u>feel</u>.

② Other ones ask you how Shakespeare makes you feel. This is sometimes called the <u>mood</u> of the scene.

Maybe Tybalt and I will be friends now...

> Act 3 Scene 1
>
> ### TASK 1
>
> From the start of this scene the audience realises the feud between the Montagues and Capulets will lead to tragedy.
>
> **Explain in detail how you think Shakespeare builds up tension and excitement in this scene.**

You need to find <u>bits</u> in the scene that <u>make you feel</u> these things.

<u>Choose</u> the Task You Can Answer Best

Once you've <u>read</u> both of the tasks through, you need to <u>make up your mind</u>. <u>Don't</u> just pick one because it <u>looks</u> like it'll be <u>less work</u> — think about how well you can answer it, too.

Pick a good 'un...

> You've <u>only</u> got to do <u>one</u> task — you need to do it as <u>well</u> as you <u>can</u>.

Picking a task — cleaning an elephant's tooth...

The secret of doing well in Paper 2 is reading <u>both tasks</u> carefully <u>before</u> you choose which one you're going to do. <u>Don't</u> just pick the one that looks easier — choose one that you can do <u>well</u>.

Section One — The basic stuff

Reading the Bit from the Play

This is the really tricky part — reading all that funny lingo. Yep — there's no way round it.

Use These Clues to Help You Read it

"More out: end Jail!"
Sounds interesting...

1) Check you've got the right play — you really don't want to get that wrong.

ROMEO AND JULIET

2) Make sure you've got the right bit too.

Act 3 Scene 5, line 37 to the end of the scene

3) This tells you who's speaking.

Enter NURSE [*hastily*]

NURSE	Madam!
JULIET	Nurse?

4) Here's what each person is saying.

5) These bits are instructions for people acting in the play — nobody actually says them.

NURSE	Your lady mother is coming to your chamber. The day is broke, be wary, look about.
JULIET	Then, window let day in, and let life out.
ROMEO	Farewell, farewell! one kiss, and I'll descend.

[*Exit*]   40

6) This is the line number.

You Must Read through the Whole Thing

It's boring, I'm afraid, but you've got to do it. You'll get around six pages to read. Don't try to skim it — you'll miss loads of important things if you do.

First, go through the passage quickly, just looking at the names of the characters and the stage directions (the bits that tell you what the characters are doing). Jot down some notes on who is in the scene and what happens — that's a good start.

Next, read through the whole thing carefully. Try to work out what it all means (Section Three is all about understanding the weird bits in the language). If you don't understand some of the scene, don't worry — come back to it later.

You'll get 15 minutes to read it and make notes — that's loads of time if you don't waste it.

I dig this play — I read the hole thing...

Don't try to cut corners. The only way you're going to write a decent answer is by reading right through the bit of the play and finding all the things you need to write about. Harsh, but true...

Working Out the Task

Hmmm — this all seems like a <u>lot of work</u> to me. It <u>doesn't</u> have to be — it's all about <u>knowing</u> what you've got to do <u>before</u> you start writing. It's the <u>only way</u> to get <u>good marks</u>.

Make Notes on Exactly What the Task is Asking For

Each task has a list of <u>handy tips</u> to help you with your answer.

> **What do you learn about the Nurse here and how does her character add to the humour in these scenes?**
>
> Before you begin to write you should think about:
>
> - the Nurse's feelings about her involvement in the secret arrangements;
> - how the different ways the Nurse speaks to Romeo and Mercutio are amusing;
> - the humour in the different ways Mercutio, Romeo and Juliet treat the Nurse;
> - how the Nurse's behaviour towards Juliet adds humour.

Make sure you scribble some <u>notes</u> on these points. You need to find <u>bits in the play</u> that <u>talk about</u> these things.

You <u>must</u> write about <u>these things</u> in your answer.

Then You've Got to Answer All the Bits of the Task

It's no good just doing <u>part</u> of the task — you've got to do <u>everything</u> they ask you to. Keep an eye out for some tasks that ask you to do <u>more than one thing</u>.

> **What similarities and differences are there between Mercutio and Tybalt and who do you think is most to blame for their deaths?**

Here's <u>one</u> question — it's about comparing Mercutio and Tybalt.

...And here's <u>another</u> — who's <u>most</u> to blame for their deaths?

Two things at once? Piece of cake...

These are the tough ones — you have to do <u>twice</u> as much to answer them properly. If you choose a task like this, make absolutely sure you do <u>both parts</u> of it.

I hate exams — always taking me to task...

It really is <u>ultra-important</u> to make sure you know what you're supposed to write about. If you don't do what the task says, you won't get the <u>marks</u>. That's the simple truth.

4 Things you Need to be Able to Do

Whatever you do, make sure you <u>learn</u> these next two pages — they'll really help your marks.

You've Got to Show You Understand the Scene

This is the secret of doing well in Paper 2 — understanding the scene you're writing about. It's the <u>only</u> possible way to do the task.

There are Four Key Things You Need to be Able to Do

(1) You've got to show you've <u>read</u> the scene and <u>know what happens</u> in it — and think about <u>why</u>.

Who do you think is most to blame for the deaths of Mercutio and Tybalt?

I blame society

You can't answer this unless you know what happens — it isn't as easy as it looks. They <u>don't</u> want you to say, "Tybalt, because he killed Mercutio, so Romeo killed him."

Instead you need to know about <u>all</u> the possibilities.

So who's <u>not</u> dead? Looks like we've found a culprit...

Act 3, Scene 1:

1) Tybalt wants to fight Romeo — he comes looking for him.
2) Mercutio starts insulting Tybalt. Romeo appears, but refuses to fight.
3) Tybalt and Mercutio think he's being a coward.
4) Mercutio decides to defend Romeo's honour by fighting Tybalt.
5) Romeo tries to break up the fight — Tybalt stabs Mercutio under Romeo's arm.
6) Mercutio dies, blaming the <u>feud</u>, and <u>Romeo</u> for getting in the way.
7) Romeo fights Tybalt and kills him in revenge for Mercutio's death.

Phew — there are <u>at least three</u> people who <u>could</u> be to blame: Romeo, Tybalt and Mercutio. Or even the feud itself! You have to write about <u>all</u> the possibilities to give a <u>good answer</u>.

> You <u>can't</u> write a <u>good</u> answer <u>unless</u> you know exactly <u>what happens</u> in the scene.

(2) You also need to show that you <u>know</u> what the <u>characters</u> are <u>like</u>.

What do you learn about the Nurse and how does her character add to the humour in these scenes?

This is all about knowing what the Nurse is like — and finding bits in the scenes they give you to <u>back up</u> what you're saying. You must give <u>examples</u> to prove you <u>know</u> what you're <u>talking about</u>.

A well-behaved communist — good Marx...

Understanding the scene — <u>that's</u> what it's all about. You have to show the examiners that you know <u>what happens</u> in the scene, and what the <u>characters</u> are like — look at Sections 4 and 5.

4 Things you Need to be Able to Do

It's not just <u>character</u> and <u>story</u> you need to know about — you need <u>moods</u> and <u>opinions</u> too.

Watch Out — These Two are Much Harder

③ You've got to be able to write about the <u>mood</u> of a scene — what it <u>feels like</u> to hear or read it — and <u>how</u> Shakespeare uses language to <u>make you</u> feel like that.

This sounds really tricky — it's all about what the scene makes <u>you feel</u>.

Feeling tents always got Brian very excited

Explain in detail how you think Shakespeare builds up tension and excitement in this scene.

<u>These</u> are the <u>feelings</u> you're looking for in the scene.
You need to look at the <u>way</u> the characters <u>speak</u> and the <u>kind of words</u> they use.

Act 1, Scene 1 doesn't start with the main characters — just Capulet's servants. This isn't what the audience expects. In fact, it's a complete change of style from the formal poetry in the prologue, since the servants don't speak poetry.

Instead, the servants make rude jokes about the Montagues. There's nothing very tense or exciting about this at all — but it's clear that the Montagues are always on their minds: "The quarrel is between our masters, and us their men."

Suddenly two servants of the Montagues appear. The mood changes immediately. It becomes tense because the quarrel isn't about words any more — now it's about real fighting. You just feel that something bad is about to happen.

> This is about the way the characters speak.

> You must give examples from the scene to back up your points.

④ You may be asked to write <u>as if</u> you were one of the <u>characters</u> in the play.

You have to try to <u>understand</u> the character, and make sure you <u>don't</u> say anything that the character <u>wouldn't know</u>.

Imagine you are Juliet writing in your diary after the argument with your parents. Write down your thoughts and feelings about being forced to marry Paris.

This is a disaster! My parents are trying to force me to marry Paris. How can I marry him? Romeo is my husband — we were married in Church. I can't marry anybody else without breaking the law, but if I don't then I'm disobeying my father's wishes. How can I tell him I'm already secretly married? How can I tell him I married the son of his great enemy?

You've got to <u>know</u> the play <u>really well</u> to be able to <u>use</u> this sort of stuff in your answer.

Mood — the way the cows spoke...

This is what it's all about — <u>knowing the play</u> really <u>well</u>. Learn it and you'll cope with <u>any task</u>.

Writing Well & Giving Examples

Two more <u>key things</u> you have to do here — make sure you get them <u>clear</u> in your head now.

You Also Get Marked on How Well You Write

1) It's painful but true — you've got to keep your <u>spelling</u> and <u>punctuation</u> as perfect as possible. They'll take marks away from you if you don't.

2) Don't forget to write in <u>paragraphs</u>. Every time you want to talk about a <u>new idea</u>, start a <u>new paragraph</u>.

3) Here's the <u>tough</u> one — you've got to try to sound <u>interested</u> in the play, even if you don't like it. Show the examiners that you're keen by using lots of <u>interesting words</u> and <u>phrases</u> in your answer.

> *Shakespeare makes your spine tingle with excitement in this scene — right from the start you know that it's going to end in a fight.*

You <u>aren't</u> marked on how well you <u>ride</u>.

You've Got to Give Loads of Examples

How many sample eggs did you want?

This is what it's all about. They want you to give <u>examples</u> from the scene that have <u>something</u> to do with the task you chose — that's your <u>answer</u>.

The <u>only</u> way to give examples is by <u>picking</u> the <u>right bits</u> from the scene. Then you need to <u>explain why</u> each bit is <u>relevant</u> — <u>how</u> it helps <u>answer</u> the question.

> You <u>won't</u> get high marks for what you write <u>unless</u> you give <u>examples</u> to <u>back it up</u>.

You Can Write About Any Versions of the Play You've Seen

In your answer, you can write about <u>any version</u> of the play you've seen, as long as it's <u>relevant</u> to the task. That includes any <u>videos</u>, <u>films</u> or <u>theatre productions</u> you've seen.

Just remember, <u>each</u> version can be very <u>different</u>. Every version has a <u>director</u> who decides what the <u>costumes</u> will look like, which <u>actors</u> will play the characters and how they'll <u>say their lines</u>.

Some directors <u>change</u> lots of things in the play — you should write about the things they <u>change</u> and the <u>way</u> they do it. Make sure you say <u>which</u> version you're talking about.

> STRANGE AND STRANGER THEATRE PRESENTS:
> ## Romeo and Juliet
> Featuring Wee Green People and Big Pink Hairdos

In the 1997 film of the play, everyone wore modern clothes. The director used loud music, guns and big explosions to show that Shakespeare could be really exciting.

Like a version — didn't Madonna sing that...

You're being marked on two things in your SAT — <u>how well</u> you <u>read</u> and <u>understand</u> the bit from the play and <u>how well</u> you <u>write</u> about it. And the secret is to give plenty of <u>examples</u>.

Revision Summary

Well, there it is. You've been catapulted into the world of Shakespeare. This first section should give you a jolly good slab of knowledge to build everything else on. It won't do you much good if you don't learn it, though. This is where these cunning Revision Summary questions come in. Do them all, don't miss any out, and keep doing them until you've got them all right. If you don't know the answers, look back through the section. Happy learning...

1) Why do the characters have funny names, like Mercutio and Benvolio?

2) What are the names of the two warring families?

3) What would happen to anyone caught fighting in the street?

4) When in the play does Romeo meet Juliet?   a) *Act One* b) *Act Two* c) *Act Three*

5) Romeo and Juliet get married. What's the name of the priest who marries them?

6) Who kills Mercutio?

7) Who kills Tybalt?

8) Who does Juliet's father want her to marry?

9) Why does Juliet feel she can't refuse her father's demand?

10) What does Juliet do when she realises this?

11) Why does Romeo decide to kill himself?

12) How does Juliet die?

13) In the SAT, how many questions will there be about *Romeo and Juliet*?

14) How many questions do you have to answer?   a) *One* b) *Two* c) *As many as you like*

15) What should you do when you read the scene through quickly?

16) What should you do next?   a) *Start writing your answer*   b) *Read the scene carefully*
   c) *Ask for a drink of water — exams are thirsty work*

17) If the task gives you four hints to "think about before you start to write," how many of the hints should you write about?   a) *None of them — they're only hints*   b) *One or two, just to show you care* c) *All four of them*

18) What are the four key things you need to do to get good marks?

19) Apart from understanding the scene, what else do you get marked on?

20) If you've seen a film or a stage production of Romeo and Juliet, are you allowed to write about it in the SAT?

Exams in the desert — thirsty work...

Why the Play Seems Weird

Lots of the things that seem weird in _Romeo and Juliet_ weren't weird when it was written. You've got to know what they are — it's the only way to answer the SAT questions properly.

Don't Forget the Play is Over 400 Years Old

Phew — that's pretty old for anything, especially a play. It's like an episode of Eastenders still being popular in the year 2400. It's not surprising that a lot of it seems strange nowadays.

Things have Changed Loads Since Then

Stuff that seems normal to us would be just as weird to Shakespeare — like regular baths...Yuk.

1) It's set in Italy, so all the names are <u>Italian</u>. They're also quite <u>old-fashioned</u>. At the time they would have sounded really exotic and exciting.

2) A lot of the things people <u>do</u> in the play are a bit odd too. When Romeo and Juliet fall in love, they decide to <u>get married</u> straightaway. In those days, that was the <u>only way</u> you could be together if you were in love. You <u>weren't</u> allowed to go out with people or live with them.

3) Then there's the fact that Juliet's parents are trying to <u>arrange</u> a marriage between her and Paris. That was actually quite <u>common</u> at the time Shakespeare was writing. Parents were loads <u>stricter</u> than they are now, and they could <u>tell</u> kids <u>what to do</u> whether they liked it or not.

Put yourself in the right frame of mind and imagine you're there.

It's Meant to be Acted — Not Just Read

1) _Romeo and Juliet_ is a play, not a book — it's meant to be seen on a <u>stage</u> with <u>actors</u> playing the parts.

2) When you read it, all you get is what the characters <u>say</u>. It's often pretty hard to <u>follow</u> what's going on.

3) You've got to try to <u>imagine</u> what's happening. Think about what the people are <u>like</u>, and how you think they would <u>speak</u> and <u>act</u>.

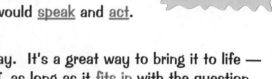

Let the words come to life....

4) If you can, watch a <u>film</u> or <u>TV version</u> of the play. It's a great way to bring it to life — and you're allowed to <u>write about it</u> in your SAT, as long as it <u>fits in</u> with the question.

Four hundred years old — I remember it Will...

This section's all about the things that make the play seem <u>strange</u> to us — and <u>why</u> they're there. You need to <u>understand</u> the things that happen in the play and find out <u>why</u> they happen.

Tricky Play Stuff

This is going to sound really obvious but it's dead important — a lot of the weird things about _Romeo and Juliet_ are there because it's a play.

It's Meant to be Watched by an Audience

The whole point of a play is it <u>tells a story</u> by <u>showing you</u> what happened. You actually get to <u>see</u> Romeo and Juliet killing themselves. Anybody <u>watching</u> the play is part of the <u>audience</u>.

As action packed as a good episode of Neighbours...

The Idea is to Make the Audience Feel Different Moods

Whew...Anyone in the mood for pizza after that...

1) The things that happen and the things people say in the play are there to make the audience feel different <u>moods</u> — swordfights get everyone <u>excited</u>, arguments get them <u>cross</u> and <u>deaths</u> might make them feel sad.

2) You'll get loads of marks in the SAT if you say what the <u>audience feels</u> about a scene. It sounds tricky but it just means saying what <u>you feel</u> when you <u>read</u> it. Don't forget to give <u>examples</u> from the scene to <u>back up</u> what you're saying.

The People in the Play are Called the Characters

The <u>characters</u> are the people in the story, like Romeo, Juliet and Benvolio. The <u>actors</u> are the people who play them — don't get them confused.

Romeo is a <u>character</u>. Leonardo Di Caprio is an <u>actor</u> who played Romeo.

The <u>main characters</u> usually speak in <u>poetry</u> — another <u>odd</u> thing about plays. See Section 3.

Sometimes They Talk to Themselves

One of the weirdest things about _Romeo and Juliet_ is when characters talk to themselves, like Juliet at the start of the balcony scene in Act 2, Scene 1, or in Act 3, Scene 2.

A bit like singing in the shower, you think you're alone, but everyone can hear you....unfortunately.

It's a way for the audience to find out what a character's <u>thinking</u> — the character just says it <u>out loud</u>.

Romeo and Juliet — a play with character...

Writing about a scene is all about what the <u>audience feels</u> when they watch it — it's a great way to <u>pick up marks</u>. Make sure you <u>learn</u> the difference between the <u>characters</u> and the <u>actors</u> too.

Tricky Play Words

This page deals with those fancy play words that keep coming up. I know they're pretty boring but you really do need to know what they mean. Make sure you learn them all carefully.

Romeo and Juliet is a Tragedy

A tragedy just means a kind of play where the main characters die at the end. Shakespeare wrote lots of tragedies but *Romeo and Juliet* is one of his most famous ones.

It'll leave you crying like a baby...

It's Divided into Acts and Scenes

1) The play is divided into five big sections, called acts. Each act is like an episode of a TV serial — lots of things happen in it, but it's only part of the whole thing.

"I love to cause a scene."

2) Each act is made up of smaller sections called scenes. There's nothing complicated about them. A scene shows you a small bit of the story and then ends. Then a new scene starts that shows you the next bit.

3) Scenes are just a way of breaking up the story. They show that time has passed in the story — one scene could be set in the evening and the next one on the following day.

4) They also let the play move to different places — one scene will happen in Capulet's house, the next one in the streets of Verona etc.

In your SAT, you'll only have to read one or two scenes from the play.

Stage Directions Say What the Characters are Doing

Stage directions are little phrases in brackets like these.

[Unlocks the door]   [They fight]

These are the really common ones:

Enter = when someone comes onto the stage

Exit = when one person leaves the stage

Exeunt = when more than one person leaves the stage

The Prologue is Like an Introduction to the Play

The bit right at the beginning of the play's called the prologue — a posh name for an introduction. It's spoken by the Chorus — a sort of storyteller. There's an introduction to Act 2 as well.

A professional dead tree — is that a pro-log...

You've got to get used to these tricky play words — they come up again and again.

The Setting of the Play

Most of the weird stuff in _Romeo and Juliet_ comes from the setting — the place where it's supposed to be happening. This page is all about <u>what</u> the setting is like, and <u>why</u> it's like that.

The Play's Set in Verona — an Italian City

Take a look into Verona and enjoy the unexpected.

1) Verona is a city in the North of Italy. In the play it's a <u>city state</u> — a sort of small independent <u>country</u>. The <u>Prince</u> of Verona rules the city like a King. He makes the <u>laws</u> and everyone <u>obeys</u> him.

2) Shakespeare probably <u>never</u> went to the real Verona — it just happens to be where the story's set. It's based on an Italian legend in an old poem.

There's a Feud between Two Families in the City

There are two powerful families in the play — the Montagues and the Capulets. They're in the middle of a <u>feud</u> — a quarrel that's lasted for years.

But zer is, somezing wrong wiz zis meat.

Feuds happen over all sorts of silly things...

It might not sound too serious to us, but it was a big deal in those days. For one thing, everybody had swords — if the two sides <u>met</u> in the street they could end up fighting a huge <u>battle</u>.

There were loads of feuds between powerful families in Italy at that time. Feuding was a <u>dangerous</u> business though — lots of people were <u>killed</u> in the fighting.

Nah mate, you're just insane!

The Feud is All About Honour

The feud's all about <u>honour</u> — the <u>respect</u> you get from other people. It's the idea that you're responsible for <u>defending</u> the things you care about, like your <u>family</u> and your <u>friends</u>.

Honour's also about having <u>pride</u> in yourself — if someone insults you, you do it right back. In the play, <u>neither</u> family will back down because they <u>hate</u> each other.

Romeo and Juliet Go Against Family Honour

This is really important for understanding the play. When Romeo and Juliet fall in <u>love</u>, they're taking a big risk. It goes <u>against</u> the whole feud. Juliet warns Romeo <u>against</u> her <u>own family</u>:

You're fish feud, mate...!

"If they do see thee, they will murder thee"
Act 2, Scene 2, line 70

It's incredibly <u>dangerous</u> for them to be together — they have to get married <u>in secret</u>.

Hungry for a fight — must have more feud...

It's all about that pesky <u>feud</u> — that's what <u>causes</u> all the <u>trouble</u> in this play. You need to keep in mind that the play is set slap-bang in the <u>middle</u> of a fight for <u>family honour</u> — it's like the <u>mafia</u>.

Honour

All this honour malarkey sounds pretty silly if you ask me — but it's a really big clue for understanding the play. It'll help you see <u>why</u> things happen the <u>way they do</u>.

Most <u>of the Characters</u> Fight <u>for Their Honour</u>

Right at the start of the play, some servants of the Montagues and Capulets meet in the street. They start insulting each other and it turns into a fight.

Fight for your honour like a man.

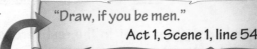

"Draw, if you be men."
Act 1, Scene 1, line 54

This means draw your swords. It's saying that anyone who <u>doesn't</u> fight for their honour <u>isn't</u> a real man — he's a coward.

I'm not fighting anyone — I'm a cow-herd.

But Anyone <u>Caught Fighting</u> will be <u>Executed</u>

Everyone else in Verona is <u>fed up</u> with the feud. All the <u>citizens</u> come out to help <u>stop</u> the fight at the beginning of Act 1. The Prince <u>orders</u> Montague and Capulet to <u>keep the peace</u> — and says that <u>anyone</u> caught <u>fighting</u> in the streets will be <u>executed</u>.

Tybalt <u>Thinks</u> Honour <u>is</u> More Important

When Tybalt finds out Romeo sneaked into a Capulet party, he thinks Romeo's <u>insulted</u> the <u>honour</u> of his family. He sends Romeo a letter <u>challenging</u> him to a <u>duel</u>.

Duels were one-on-one swordfights — they were fashionable for young men who wanted to show off their fighting skills.

Romeo <u>Refuses to</u> Fight Him

1)   Romeo doesn't <u>want</u> to fight Tybalt because he's just got <u>married</u> to Juliet — Tybalt is one of her relatives. Romeo loves Juliet — he doesn't want to kill her family any more.

Come on Romeo, fight like a man..

"I do protest I never injured thee,
But love thee better than thou canst devise,"
Act 3, Scene 1, lines 65-66

Always thought Tybalt had an identity crisis.

2)   Here he's saying he loves Tybalt more than Tybalt knows — because he's part of the <u>same family</u> now.

<u>No one</u> understands <u>why</u> Romeo won't fight. They <u>don't know</u> about the wedding — they think he's being a <u>coward</u>.

Duels — who wants to have a stab at them...

When you write about a scene you've got to be able to say <u>why</u> the characters do what they do, or the examiners <u>won't think</u> that you've <u>understood</u> it. Remember characters are <u>fighting</u> for <u>honour</u>.

<u>*Honour*</u>

Honour is the reason for the feud — and even though Romeo wants to <u>escape</u> it, he <u>can't</u>.

<u>Mercutio Fights to Defend Romeo's Honour</u>

When Romeo refuses to fight Tybalt, his best friend Mercutio can't believe it.

> "O calm, dishonourable, vile submission!"
> (Act 3, Scene 1, line 70)

He doesn't know Romeo's married Juliet — and he thinks Romeo's <u>lost</u> his self-respect. Mercutio decides to <u>fight Tybalt</u> instead.

<u>The Fight Ends in His Death — By Mistake</u>

When Tybalt and Mercutio start fighting, Romeo tries to break them up — he moves between them and Tybalt stabs Mercutio under Romeo's arm.

<u>Romeo Can't Escape the Feud — It Ruins Everything</u>

1) This is one of the most <u>important bits</u> in the whole play. Even though Romeo tries to <u>stay out</u> of the feud, and tries to <u>stop</u> any fighting, Mercutio <u>still</u> gets <u>killed</u>.

2) It's worse because Mercutio is the <u>first person</u> to die in the play — and he <u>isn't</u> a Montague or a Capulet. It shows how <u>pointless</u> the feud is — it causes the death of someone who <u>isn't</u> involved.

Now Look what you've done Romeo...

> "A plague a' both your houses!"
> (Act 3, Scene 1, line 101)

3) Mercutio <u>blames</u> both the <u>Montagues</u> and the <u>Capulets</u>. He also <u>blames Romeo</u> for getting in the way.

4) Mercutio <u>dies</u> and Romeo is <u>furious</u> — he's desperate for <u>revenge</u> so he <u>kills</u> Tybalt.

5) Now he has killed a <u>Capulet</u> — he's <u>made the feud</u> between the families even <u>worse</u>. There's <u>no way</u> he'll be <u>accepted</u> as Juliet's husband — the feud has <u>ruined</u> his chances.

6) When the Prince arrives, he <u>banishes</u> Romeo from Verona — he <u>won't</u> even be able to see Juliet <u>in secret</u>, all because of that terrible feud.

<u>*Mercutio — always dying to help Romeo...*</u>

<u>Honour</u> and the <u>feud</u> — they're the two things that Romeo <u>can't escape</u>. Even when he's married to Juliet and everything seems to be alright, that feud <u>causes trouble</u>. You've got to know <u>how</u>.

Family & Marriage

OK, this is where a lot of things have changed since Shakespeare's time. You've got to remember that lots of these things <u>weren't</u> strange then although they seem <u>really odd</u> now.

The Capulets Want to Arrange Juliet's Marriage

In the play, Count Paris wants to marry Juliet — he's a rich and powerful noble.
Right at the start of the play, Capulet's trying to <u>set them up</u>.

Marriage Wasn't for Love — but for Money

1) In the 16th century, when the play was written, rich people like the Capulets or Montagues <u>didn't</u> get married for <u>love</u>. Their parents arranged a marriage with someone rich or powerful. It was a <u>business deal</u> — a way of getting more money and power into the family.

2) In *Romeo and Juliet*, Juliet is Lord Capulet's only heir — when he dies she gets all his money and property. But if she gets married, her <u>husband</u> would get all that money.

3) Normally the two people getting married <u>didn't</u> get much of a <u>say</u>. They were <u>told</u> they <u>had</u> to get married and <u>who</u> they were marrying.

But Juliet is Only Thirteen

This is where it gets really odd — Juliet is <u>only</u> 13 in the play. At first Capulet says she's far <u>too young</u> to be getting married.

> "Let two more summers wither in their pride
> Ere we may think her ripe to be a bride."
> (Act 1, Scene 2, lines 10-11)

What... does he think I'm a piece of fruit?

He also says that Juliet should <u>have a say</u> in whether she marries Paris.

This is quite tricky — it means "if she agrees to marry you, I'll agree too."

> "And she agreed, within her scope of choice
> Lies my consent and fair according voice."
> (Act 1, Scene 2, lines 18-19)

After Tybalt dies, Juliet is really upset because Romeo has been <u>banished</u>. Capulet thinks she's upset because of Tybalt, and tries to <u>force</u> her to marry Paris.

> "I tell thee what: get thee to church on Thursday,
> Or never after look me in the face."
> (Act 3, Scene 5, lines 161-2)

Cowboy weddings — a-range-d marriages...

Juliet's thirteen and her parents want to make her marry someone — blimey. It's a completely different world. That's what you've got to get into your head — it isn't like nowadays at all.

Why Life is Hard for Juliet

Juliet has it pretty tough in *Romeo and Juliet* — she doesn't get any choices about her life.
When she falls in love with Romeo, it seems like she's escaped — until things start going wrong.

Juliet is Supposed to Do What She's Told

1) Juliet's parents <u>don't</u> really <u>know</u> her very well — they don't have much clue about what she wants, and they <u>don't</u> really <u>care</u>. For <u>most</u> of her life, she's been brought up by the <u>Nurse</u>.

I know how you feel..

2) Juliet <u>isn't</u> even allowed out of the house <u>without</u> permission. She has to <u>send the Nurse</u> to take messages to Romeo — she <u>can't</u> go herself.

3) <u>Capulet</u> is in complete <u>control</u> of his family — he can tell Juliet to marry whoever <u>he wants</u>. She <u>isn't</u> supposed to <u>marry</u> anyone <u>without</u> his permission.

There are Two Problems When She Marries Romeo

① Here's the obvious one — Romeo's a Montague and she's a Capulet. Both of them are going <u>against</u> the <u>feud</u> and <u>against</u> their <u>family's honour</u> by marrying an <u>enemy</u>.

② Juliet's <u>disobeying</u> her parents — they want her to marry Paris, but she's marrying Romeo for <u>love</u>. They have to get married in <u>secret</u>.

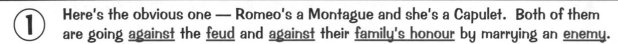
Verona is full of <u>hate</u> — the only <u>real love</u> in the play is between Romeo and Juliet, but it <u>doesn't survive</u> for very long.

It's all going a little pear shaped.

How Things Get Worse After They're Married

You really need to get this part straight. Unless you understand <u>how</u> things go wrong for Romeo and Juliet, you <u>won't</u> be able to give <u>clear answers</u> about any scenes after Act 3.

Cheer up mate, things could be worse, you could be a frog.

① Romeo <u>kills</u> Tybalt and gets <u>banished</u> — he <u>won't</u> be able to see Juliet.

② Capulet tells Juliet she <u>has to</u> marry Paris. If she <u>doesn't</u>, then he says he'll <u>throw her out</u>.

③ Juliet <u>can't</u> marry him — she's <u>already married</u> to Romeo. If she <u>marries</u> Paris, she'll be <u>breaking</u> a sacred <u>promise</u> to Romeo — and <u>breaking the law</u>.

The bride's favouwite colour — wed, pewhaps

Blimey — Juliet has a <u>hard time</u> in the play. You need to know <u>why</u>. Make sure you <u>learn</u> the <u>two problems</u> Romeo and Juliet face, and how things <u>get worse</u> after they get married.

Religion

Religion plays a really big part in the play — it'll help you understand <u>why</u> the characters do some of the weird things they do.

The Church <u>was</u> Really Powerful in the 16th Century

In Shakespeare's time, everybody had to go to Church on Sunday — if you didn't you were made to pay a fine. <u>No one</u> could get married <u>except</u> in Church — and no couple could <u>be together unless</u> they got married.

> Juliet <u>insists</u> on getting <u>married</u> because it's the <u>only way</u> she can <u>be with Romeo</u>.

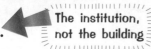

Don't worry, we'll be safe in here.

The Friar Gives Confidential Advice

Romeo and Juliet both go to the Friar for advice. There are <u>two good reasons</u> for this:

I must confess, you are a handsome man

1) People can go to a priest or a friar for <u>confession</u> — they can tell the priest all their secrets, so he can give them advice. The Friar <u>isn't</u> allowed to tell anyone else about the secrets — Romeo and Juliet can <u>trust</u> him.

2) They are going <u>against</u> their families and friends — the Friar is the only person they can talk to who <u>isn't involved</u> in the feud. They can't talk to their parents.

Romeo and Juliet's Marriage <u>is</u> Protected by the Church

Marriage is <u>sacred</u> to the Church — once Romeo and Juliet are married by the Friar, they are under the protection of the Church.

The institution, not the building

It would be a <u>sin</u> for Juliet to marry Paris — breaking the law of the Church, because she's already married.

It's one of the reasons why the Friar helps Romeo and Juliet.

Romeo Gets Sanctuary After Killing Tybalt

When Romeo's killed Tybalt, he goes straight to Friar Lawrence. That's because the Friar's the <u>only</u> person who's on his and Juliet's side.

There's another reason too though. When someone <u>committed a crime</u>, they could go to the Church and ask for <u>sanctuary</u> — the <u>Church's protection</u>.

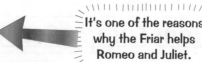

If your name's not down, you're not coming in....

They would be safe as long as they did what the Church told them.

Romeo & Juliet — a marriage made in heaven...

This <u>religion</u> stuff is a really important thing in the play. Romeo and Juliet <u>have to</u> get married, otherwise their love doesn't <u>mean</u> anything to them. Make sure you can explain the <u>Friar's role</u>.

Revision Summary

It's a funny old play <u>Romeo and Juliet</u> — that's why it's important to get this section down in your head. There are two big things to get sorted — all the stuff about plays, and all that business about the setting. Just remember the best way to test what you know is to have a go at a few questions. You know it makes sense.

1) Where is the play set?

2) What is the point of a play?

3) What is an audience?

4) How does the play create different moods?

5) Who are the characters of the play?

6) What's the difference between characters and actors?

7) Why do people talk to themselves in the play?

8) What is an Act?

9) What is a scene?

10) What are the stage directions?

11) What is the prologue?

12) What is a feud?

13) How do Romeo and Juliet go against family honour?

14) Why does Romeo refuse to fight Tybalt?

15) How old is Juliet in the play?

16) Why does Capulet try to force her to marry Paris?

17) What are the two big problems when Juliet marries Romeo?

18) Give three reasons why things get worse after they're married.

19) Why can Romeo and Juliet trust the Friar?

20) What does sanctuary mean?

Why the Language is Hard

Everyone says Shakespeare's plays are brilliant — but they're a <u>nightmare</u> to understand.
Or at least they <u>seem</u> that way until you get a few things <u>clear</u> in your head.

Watch Out — The Language Looks Really Tricky

1) Shakespeare's language looks <u>hard</u> — but there's <u>no way round</u> it, I'm afraid. You'll be given a <u>scene</u> to read in your SAT — and you've <u>got</u> to be able to <u>understand</u> what happens, or you won't get <u>any marks</u> at all.

Curses — there's no getting round this thing!

Shakespeare's Language

2) <u>Don't worry</u> if you can't understand <u>anything</u> to start with. Read a scene <u>a few times</u>, and you'll be surprised how much <u>does</u> make sense once you get <u>used to it</u>.

3) Don't forget — it was <u>meant</u> to be spoken out <u>loud</u>. Try reading some of it out loud with your mates — some things may become <u>clear</u> that weren't before.

There's <u>no point</u> in <u>worrying</u> about how hard it is — just <u>get on</u> and <u>learn how</u> to <u>read</u> it.

Some of the Play's in Poetry — Some Isn't

<u>Romeo and Juliet</u> is written in a mixture of <u>poetry</u> and <u>prose</u> — prose is any kind of language that <u>isn't</u> poetry.

Poetry in Motion?

① Here's how to <u>spot</u> a bit of <u>poetry</u>.

<u>Every line</u> starts with a <u>capital letter</u>.

> O Lord, I could have stay'd here all the night
> To hear good counsel. O, what learning is!
> Act 3, Scene 3, 159-160

<u>Sometimes</u> the last word of a line <u>rhymes</u> with the last word of the <u>next one</u>.

> Could we but learn from whence his sorrows grow,
> We would as willingly give cure as know.
> Act 1, Scene 1, 145-6

② Any bits where the lines run on normally, <u>without</u> extra capitals or rhymes, are in <u>prose</u>.

> A gentleman, nurse, that loves to hear himself talk, and will speak
> more in a minute than he will stand to in a month.
> Act 2, Scene 4, 123-4

There's <u>no</u> capital letter.

I like poetry — I've weighed up the prose and cons...

The secret of this language stuff is just <u>getting used</u> to it. It's never going to get any easier unless you <u>read</u> the play lots. Sounds boring, I know, but it's the <u>only way</u> to <u>work out</u> what's going on.

Poetry In The Play

Some of the play is in poetry, and some of it's in prose. Shakespeare was doing it on purpose, it really helps you understand what's going on if you know why. Read on.

This Prose and Poetry Stuff Isn't Just for Fun

It was all deliberate!

1) Writing most of it in poetry makes it easier to use loads of fancy words and images — which make the play interesting and clever.

2) Whether people are speaking in poetry or prose tells you if they're posh or common, and if they're talking seriously or just joking around.

3) Back in the 15th century, the difference would've been tons more obvious — like hearing posh or common accents is obvious nowadays.

Sometimes the Play Definitely Has to Be in POETRY...

① The main characters all speak in poetry most of the time. Shakespeare's using the poetry to make them seem grand — they're all posh nobles.

> PRINCE: You, Capulet, shall go along with me,
> And, Montague, come you this afternoon,
> Act 1, Scene 1, 90-91

10 or 11 syllables in each line.

> PARIS: Madam, good night, commend me to your daughter.
> LADY C: I will, and know her mind early tomorrow.
> Act 3, Scene 4, 9-10

A capital letter at the start of every line.

I am dead posh me, So I speak in poetry.

Anybody who has any authority in the play speaks poetry — like when the Prince gives judgement, or Capulet tells Juliet she must marry Paris. Friar Lawrence also speaks poetry — he's got authority as an adviser to Romeo and Juliet.

This is part of a love scene between Romeo and Juliet — it's in poetry.

② If a whole scene is in poetry, then it's either a love scene between Romeo and Juliet with lots of pretty images, or it's a formal scene between the posh characters.

> JULIET: Believe me, love, it was the nightingale.
> ROMEO: It was the lark, the herald of the morn,
> Act 3, Scene 5, 5-6

...and Sometimes it Absolutely Must Be in PROSE

1) Common characters always speak in prose — like the Nurse, and the servants.

This is in prose.

> NURSE: Is it good den?
> MERCUTIO: 'Tis no less, I tell ye, for the bawdy hand of the dial is now upon the prick of noon.
> Act 2, Scene 4, 91-3

2) Any bits of comedy in the play are in prose — even if it's the main characters speaking. Romeo and Mercutio speak prose in Act 2, Scene 2 — they're teasing the Nurse and making dirty jokes.

Speaking poetry — I'm not a-verse to it myself...

OK, that's poetry and prose. Common people speak prose, and posh people speak poetry. Get that tucked away in the grey mass between your ears. It really is worth learning.

How To Read The Poetry

Everyone <u>goes on</u> about Shakespeare's <u>poetry</u> being so flippin' marvellous — but they <u>never</u> tell you <u>how to read it</u> so it makes <u>sense</u>. That's what this page is all about — it's the <u>only way</u> you'll be able to <u>understand</u> what he's banging on about.

The <u>Secret</u> of <u>Reading the Poetry is</u> <u>Counting to Ten</u>

Before you start thinking I've gone barmy, have a look at what I mean.

<u>Every line</u> of poetry in the play has got <u>ten</u> or <u>eleven</u> syllables — or beats.

1 2   3 4 5   6   7   8   9   10

In fair Verona, where we lay our scene

They give the poetry its rhythm — dee-dum dee-dum dee-dum dee-dum dee-dum.

It sounds really stupid when you write it down, but if you <u>learn</u> it, it'll help you read the poetry much better.

It's got rhythm Maaaaaaan...

Shakespeare <u>Fiddles</u> <u>with the Words to</u> <u>Make Them Fit</u>

This is what makes the poetry tricky to read — Shakespeare fiddles with the words to make them <u>fit</u> into lines of <u>ten</u> or <u>eleven</u> syllables.

Look out for these squiggles — they <u>show you</u> when there's an extra syllable in a word.

1 Sometimes he makes a word <u>last</u> for an <u>extra syllable</u>.

> Profaners of this neighbour-stainèd steel —
> Act 1, Scene 1, 73

Normally "stained" has one syllable — but here you have to say it "stain - ed" so that there are ten syllables in the line.

2 He often <u>runs two words together</u> if he wants to <u>lose</u> a syllable.

> Trust to't, bethink you, I'll not be forsworn.
> Act 3, Scene 5, 195

This is a <u>short form</u> of "<u>to it</u>" — Shakespeare's stuck them together to make one word.

3 Worst of all, he even leaves <u>whole words</u> out — what a pain.

> Hie you to church, I must another way.
> Act 2, Scene 5, 71

"I must another way" <u>doesn't</u> seem to make any sense — Shakespeare's <u>left out</u> the word "go" so the line only has <u>ten syllables</u>.

Making words fit — dieting and exercise...

<u>Every</u> line of poetry in the play has <u>ten</u> or <u>eleven</u> syllables — <u>learn</u> that and the rest'll start to follow.

How To Read The Poetry

Phew — this poetry lark can all get a bit <u>confusing</u> at times. Make sure you get all of this <u>clear</u>.

Don't Stop *Reading at the* End *of Each Line*

Here's a simple point — but it's one you <u>mustn't</u> ever forget.

1) Even though each line starts with a capital letter, it <u>doesn't</u> mean it's a separate sentence. Just <u>ignore</u> the capitals and follow the <u>punctuation</u>.

> And to say truth, Verona brags of him
> To be a virtuous and well-govern'd youth.
> Act 1, Scene 5, 66-7

2) There's <u>no full stop</u> here so carry on to the next line.

3) There <u>isn't</u> a <u>break</u> in the sentence even when it moves to the <u>next line</u>. You've got to <u>read</u> it as if it's written like <u>this</u>:

> And to say truth, Verona brags of him to be a virtuous and well govern'd youth.

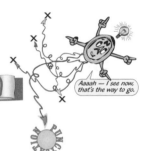

Aaaah — I see now, that's the way to go.

<u>Follow</u> the <u>punctuation</u> not the lines — or none of it'll <u>make sense</u>.

Look Out for *Long Sentences* With *Funny Word Orders*

Another big reason why the poetry's so <u>tricky</u> to understand is because there are lots of really <u>long sentences</u>. It takes ages to <u>work out</u> exactly what they mean if you don't know this stuff.

1 Here's a typical sentence — it looks dead <u>complicated</u>.

> Two households, both alike in dignity,
> In fair Verona, where we lay our scene,
> From ancient grudge break to new mutiny,
> Where civil blood makes civil hands unclean.
> Prologue, 1-4

2 It's difficult because it's in a <u>funny order</u>. This is how it should go.

> In fair Verona, where we lay our scene, two households, both alike in dignity, break to new mutiny from ancient grudge, where civil blood makes civil hands unclean.

3 It isn't clear yet, but it's getting there. <u>Modernise</u> a few words, and you get this:

> In pretty Verona, where our play takes place, two households, of the same social standing, break into a quarrel that comes from an old grudge, and cause a civil war to stain the hands of the citizens with blood.

4 Talk about <u>tough</u> to understand — but <u>don't panic</u>. The <u>more</u> of the play you read, the <u>easier</u> these sentences get.

You words have been proven to be drunken and disorderly there is nothing humorous or funny about such word order — and I shall be handing out long sentences to one and all...........

This bit is <u>back-to-front</u> — it <u>sounds</u> hard because the word order's <u>confusing</u>.

> Thy fault our law calls death, but the kind Prince,
> Taking thy part, hath rush'd aside the law,
> Act 3, Scene 3, 25-6

= Our law calls thy fault death

Shakespeare & judges — they both like long sentences...

Hurrah — another page done. <u>Don't worry</u> if it doesn't seem to be getting any easier straightaway — you'll only get better with <u>time</u> and <u>practice</u>. All this stuff is here to help you <u>work it out</u>.

Different Kinds Of Poetry

I can't say this is the most exciting stuff in the world — but it'll really <u>boost</u> your <u>marks</u>.
Some <u>SAT tasks</u> will ask you to talk about <u>how</u> Shakespeare <u>uses language</u>, so it's worth <u>learning</u>.

Most of the Play's in Blank Verse

Blank verse means bits of poetry that don't rhyme.

You can tell they're <u>poetry</u> because each <u>line</u> starts with a <u>capital letter</u>. You can also
tell from the number of <u>syllables</u> in each line — yep, you've guessed it, <u>ten</u> or <u>eleven</u>.

Here's 2 lines of blank verse.

> And to say truth, Verona brags of him
> To be a virtuous and well-governed youth.
> Act 1, Scene 5, 66-7

This gets really hairy when <u>two people</u> are talking.
Their <u>conversation</u> has to <u>fit</u> into lines of poetry.

This is <u>one line</u> with eleven syllables.

You know — since we started talking about poetry you've got an awful lot hairier.

> BALTHASAR: It doth so, holy sir, and there's my master,
> One that you love.
> FRIAR: Who is it?
> BALTHASAR: Romeo.
> FRIAR: How long hath he been there?
> BALTHASAR: Full half an hour.
> Act 5, Scene 3, 128-130

<u>All</u> of these bits form <u>one line</u> of <u>ten syllables</u> — that's why they're written like this.

These two bits together form another line.

Some Bits of it Rhyme

Some scenes in the play are <u>all</u> in rhyming lines — each line <u>rhymes</u> with the next one.
Other scenes have <u>bits</u> of rhyme in them — especially at the <u>end</u> of the scene.

Here's the end of the whole play.

> For never was a story of more woe
> Than this of Juliet and her Romeo.
> Act 5, Scene 3, 309-10

Woah there Juliet baby!

Who's he calling Juliet — how many times do I have to tell him my name's Vera?..??

Rodeo Romeo... a story of woah..!

A Few Bits are Sonnets

A couple of bits of the play are in <u>sonnets</u>.
<u>Sonnets</u> are a kind of poem with <u>fourteen lines</u>.
Shakespeare wrote <u>loads</u> of other sonnets <u>as well as</u> the ones in the play.

> The <u>Prologue</u> is a sonnet — so is the <u>Chorus's speech</u> at the <u>start</u> of Act 2.
> The <u>first fourteen lines</u> Romeo and Juliet <u>say</u> to <u>each other</u> in Act 1 Scene 5 are a sonnet too.

Poetic justice — the punishment fits the rhyme...

It <u>isn't</u> just about Shakespeare writing poetry — it's about the <u>kinds of poetry</u> he uses in different
scenes. You need to be able to <u>recognise</u> each kind so you can <u>write</u> about them in your SAT.

Old Words

Well you might think poetry was bad enough — but the play's full of <u>old words</u> as well.
And when I say old, I mean <u>old</u>...

Mind Your Thee, Thou and Thy

These <u>three words</u> turn up all the time —
they make sentences <u>look</u> much <u>harder</u> than they really are.

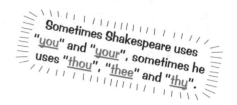
Sometimes Shakespeare uses "<u>you</u>" and "<u>your</u>", sometimes he uses "<u>thou</u>", "<u>thee</u>" and "<u>thy</u>".

Thou = You   Thee = You   Thy = Your

Thou knowest the mask of night is on my face,
Act 2, Scene 2, 85

I take thee at thy word.
Act 2, Scene 2, 49

How to look harder than you really are...

They're just an <u>old way</u> of saying <u>you</u> and <u>your</u>.
Watch out for the verbs that go with them too.

wert thou = were you

thou wilt = you will

See thee — I'll have thee I will! I'm well hard — thou'll not stand a chance.

thou hast = you have

thou swear'st = you swear

Any verbs ending in <u>-st</u> or <u>-est</u> definitely go with <u>thou</u>.
They <u>look difficult</u> but really they <u>aren't</u>.

Here are Some Common Old Words

"<u>Whence</u>" means "from where" and "<u>thence</u>" means "from there".

1) hie = go

2) hence = from here

Then hie you hence.
Act 2, Scene 5, 67

3) ere = before

I wonder at this haste, that I must wed
Ere he that should be husband comes to woo.
Act 3, Scene 5, 118-9

4) hither = to here

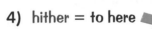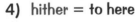
Da Woo-tang Klan

How camest thou hither,
Act 2, Scene 2, 62

It means "<u>why</u> are you Romeo" not "where".

5) wherefore = for what reason/why

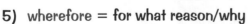
To-woo or not to-woo — that is the question...

O Romeo, Romeo, wherefore art thou Romeo?
Act 2, Scene 2, 33

Old words — Grandma, Grandpa, pension...

There are <u>lots</u> of old words in _Romeo and Juliet_ — but most of them <u>aren't</u> as scary as they look.
Just remember that <u>thee</u>, <u>thou</u> and <u>thy</u> mean you or your, and <u>learn</u> the <u>common old words</u>.

Images In The Play

This play's full of <u>images</u> — some people say they're there to make the language <u>rich</u> and <u>interesting</u>. I think they just make it a lot <u>trickier to follow</u>.

Learn _these_ Four Kinds _of_ Image _to_ Look Out For

Images are just <u>word pictures</u> — they help you see what Shakespeare's describing.

① <u>Similes</u> are when one thing is <u>like</u> something else.

> But old folks — many feign as they were dead,
> Unwieldy, slow, heavy, and pale as lead.
> Act 2, Scene 5, 16-17

This one's saying old people are <u>pale like lead</u>.

② <u>Epic similes</u> are like <u>similes</u> — they're just longer. Instead of changing the image, Shakespeare goes into <u>more and more detail</u> about the <u>same</u> image.

> My bounty is as boundless as the sea,
> My love as deep; the more I give to thee,
> The more I have, for both are infinite.
> Act 2, Scene 2, 133-5

Juliet's <u>comparing</u> her love to the <u>sea</u> — the whole thing is about the <u>same image</u>.

③ A <u>metaphor</u> is when he says one thing <u>is</u> something else. Usually it just means using <u>exaggerated language</u> to <u>describe</u> things.

It <u>doesn't</u> mean <u>actually</u> wounded — it means Romeo has fallen in love and it <u>feels like</u> he's been wounded.

> Where on a sudden one hath wounded me
> That's by me wounded;
> Act 2, Scene 3, 50-51

④ <u>Personification</u> means describing a thing <u>as if</u> it were a <u>person</u>.

"Young affection" is described like a <u>greedy son</u>, waiting for his father to <u>die</u> so he can take his place — talk about a <u>weird idea</u>.

Here "old desire" is described as a <u>dying old man</u>.

> Now old desire does in his death-bed lie,
> And young affection gapes to be his heir
> Act 2, Chorus, 1-2

Ouch — enough already that really hurts, this isn't funny...

Shakespeare's images — posh bard, sporty bard...

Hmmm — images don't half sound dull when you talk about them like this. Thing is, if you can <u>spot</u> different images when you're <u>reading</u> a scene, you'll pick up <u>loads of marks</u> for writing about them.

Common Images

Some images <u>turn up</u> time and again <u>all the way through</u> the play — you need to be able to <u>spot</u> them in any scene you're reading. Believe me, it'll make a <u>big difference</u> to your marks.

Watch Out for Light and Dark Images

<u>*Romeo and Juliet*</u> has loads of images of light and dark — especially images <u>comparing</u> them.

> JULIET: O now be gone, more light and light it grows.
> ROMEO: More light and light, more dark and dark our woes!
> Act 3, Scene 5, 35-6

He's comparing the <u>light</u> of day to the <u>darkness</u> of their problems.

This bit's about Juliet's beauty <u>lighting up</u> the <u>dark tomb</u>.

> For here lies Juliet, and her beauty makes
> This vault a feasting presence full of light.
> Act 5, Scene 3, 85-6

There are Tons of Sea Images too

> Woh, I like, see images.

1) This one's about life being like a <u>ship</u> on the sea — Romeo's asking to be <u>guided</u> in the <u>right direction</u> in the future.

> But He that hath the steerage of my course
> Direct my sail!
> Act 1, Scene 4, 112-3

2) At the <u>end</u> of the play, Romeo uses the <u>same image</u>, but now he asks to be guided <u>onto the rocks</u>. He believes Juliet is dead and he <u>wants to die</u>.

> Thou desperate pilot, now at once run on
> The dashing rocks thy sea-sick weary bark!
> Act 5, Scene 3, 117-8

> Wo... o...ooof

> Now that's one weary bark.

A <u>bark</u> is a type of little boat.

3) There are also lots of <u>storm</u> images — like this one Capulet uses to describe Juliet. He says she's so <u>upset</u> that she's like a boat in a storm... any minute she could <u>capsize</u>.

> In one little body
> Thou counterfeits a bark, a sea, a wind:
> For still thy eyes, which I may call the sea,
> Do ebb and flow with tears; the bark thy body is,
> Sailing in this salt flood; the winds, thy sighs,
> Who, raging with thy tears, and they with them,
> Without a sudden calm, will overset
> The tempest-tossèd body.
> Act 3, Scene 5, 130-7

Dark images — I always wear black...

<u>Light and dark</u> and the <u>sea</u> — watch out for these fellas. You'll be surprised — they turn up <u>a lot</u>.

More Common Images

Nearly done with this section — but there are a few more images that you'll <u>keep on meeting</u> in the play... Yep — you really do need to <u>learn</u> what they are so you can spot 'em in the SAT.

There's Lots of Stuff about Stars and Fate

It's a bit like <u>astrology</u> — the play's got loads of images about the <u>stars</u> controlling the <u>future</u>.

> From forth the fatal loins of these two foes
> A pair of star-cross'd lovers take their life;
> Prologue, 5-6

I'm afraid it must be a black hole.

IT'S NOT IT'S A SUPER NOVA!

A pair of cross star lovers

This is a dead famous phrase about Romeo and Juliet — it means they were <u>doomed</u> right from the <u>start</u>.

Here's another bit which is on about the same thing — Romeo's saying that the <u>future</u> is hanging in the <u>stars</u>, waiting to happen.

> I fear too early, for my mind misgives
> Some consequence yet hanging in the stars
> Shall bitterly begin his fearful date
> With this night's revels,
> Act 1, Scene 4, 106-9

In this bit from the <u>end</u> of the play, Romeo's about to kill himself — he wants to be free from his <u>unlucky stars</u>.

> And shake the yoke of inauspicious stars
> From this world-wearied flesh.
> Act 5, Scene 3, 111-2

"<u>Inauspicious</u>" means unlucky.

And Don't Forget the Flowers

Shakespeare always sticks lots of <u>flower</u> images in — usually about Juliet.

This is a really clear image of <u>death</u> — like frost on a flower.

> Death lies on her like an untimely frost
> Upon the sweetest flower of all the field.
> Act 4, Scene 5, 28-9

It's a pleasure to watch you work Mr Shakespeare.

There's nothing to it. I just stick a few flower images in.

When Paris comes to visit Juliet's grave, he brings flowers and <u>calls her</u> a flower too.

> Sweet flower, with flowers thy bridal bed I strew.
> Act 5, Scene 3, 12

Romeo and Juliet — more stars than Hollywood...

<u>Spotting</u> the images — that's the secret of <u>writing well</u> about Shakespeare's <u>language</u>. It's all about how he makes you <u>feel</u> different <u>moods</u> in different scenes — which is really all about the <u>images</u>.

Puns & Jokes

You might not think so, but _Romeo and Juliet_ is full of jokes. Mind you, they <u>aren't</u> very funny —
they're mostly based on words with <u>two meanings</u>.

Jokes <u>with</u> Double Meanings <u>are called</u> Puns

Shakespeare loved puns — his plays are <u>full</u> of them. They were really <u>popular</u> at
the time he was writing, because they showed how <u>clever</u> you were.

1) Sometimes they're meant to be <u>jokes</u>:

> This means "if we're angry, we'll draw our swords".

> SAMSON: I mean, and we be in choler, we'll draw.
> GREGORY: Ay, while you live, draw your neck out of a collar.
> Act 1, Scene 1, 3-4

> But this means "keep your head out
> of a noose (a hangman's "collar")".

Draw a sword?

Gregory's making a <u>pun</u> on the words "choler" (anger) and "collar" (noose) —
<u>don't</u> say I didn't warn you about them <u>not</u> being funny.

2) They can also be <u>part</u> of an <u>image</u>:

At the end of the play, Montague promises to put up a <u>gold statue</u> of Juliet.

£50000000000000000

What an amazing statue.   _A very impressive figure._

> There shall no figure at such rate be set
> As that of true and faithful Juliet.
> Act 5, Scene 3, 301-2

He's making puns on the words "<u>figure</u>" and "<u>rate</u>" — the sentence means
"no person will be respected so highly as Juliet", but it also means "no statue
will be worth so much money as Juliet's". It's about <u>money</u> as well as <u>love</u>.

3) <u>Mercutio</u> makes lots of puns —
<u>even</u> when he's dying.

He's making a pun about "grave" meaning <u>serious</u>,
and the "grave" he'll be <u>buried in</u> tomorrow.

> Ask for me tomorrow, and you shall find me a grave man.
> Act 3, Scene 1, 93

Have you heard the one about the vomiting aardvark?

Now that's a sick joke.

It's a really <u>sick joke</u> — instead of being funny, it's
incredibly <u>sad</u>. Mercutio's a <u>fun person</u> and a <u>great joker</u>,
but all of a sudden he's <u>dying</u>.

A play on words — Romeo & Juliet Play Scrabble...

They may <u>not</u> be very <u>funny</u>, but they pop up all over the shop. The play is full of <u>puns</u> — and if you
can <u>spot</u> them in a scene, you'll <u>get marks</u> for writing about them. Think about <u>why</u> they're there too.

Revision Summary

The language stuff is all pretty important — you've got to be able to read the scene properly if you're going to write about it. I know the poetry bits aren't much fun, but they're bound to come in handy. Make sure you can spot the main kinds of image in the play too — they'll show the Examiners you really understand the language. Have a go at these revision questions — they're here to help you test yourself.

1)   How do you spot a bit of poetry?

2)   Give some reasons why some of the play is in poetry.

3)   Give three kinds of situation where Shakespeare uses poetry in the play.

4)   How many syllables does each line of poetry have?

5)   Give two ways that Shakespeare fiddles with words to make them fit the line.

6)   Why musn't you stop reading at the end of each line?

7)   What three kinds of poetry are there in the play?

8)   What is blank verse?

9)   What is a sonnet?

10) What does 'thou' mean?

11) What does 'thy' mean?

12) What does 'whence' mean?

13) What does 'wherefore' mean?

14) Give three common images in the play.

15) What are puns?

Don't worry —
spear shaking has always been confusing ...

Cavemen shook their spears and did the funky wild-thing to bamboozle their prey

Who's Who in the Play

There are loads of characters in the play, with all sorts of tricky names.
The main ones are on this page. It's easy to get muddled — so go through this carefully.

These are the Capulets

LORD CAPULET

LADY CAPULET

JULIET

TYBALT
Juliet's cousin

And These are the Montagues

LORD MONTAGUE

LADY MONTAGUE

ROMEO

BENVOLIO
Romeo's cousin

These Three Characters are Related Too

COUNT PARIS
*Capulet wants to arrange a marriage
between Paris and Juliet*

THE PRINCE
ruler of Verona

MERCUTIO
Romeo's best friend

Two Characters Who Play a Big Part in the Marriage

NURSE
*Juliet's servant, takes
messages between
Romeo and Juliet*

FRIAR LAWRENCE
*arranges Juliet and Romeo's
wedding, gives Juliet
potion to fake her death*

What's in a name? Marks — so learn them...

Shakespeare didn't half give his characters some funny old names. Use this page to learn the names and who's related to who. It'll make things one heck of a lot easier in the long run.

Romeo

You need to do a bit more than remember Romeo's name. If you learn a few points about what he's like, you can look out for them in the scene you get in the test.

Romeo's a Lover and a Killer

Romeo's a romantic dreamer... but he's got a more dangerous side too — he's not afraid to fight to the death.

Romeo's the only son of the Montagues, a noble Verona family. They're fighting a feud with the Capulets. It's almost impossible for Romeo to avoid getting involved in fights, because of the feud.

It's more difficult to be a lover. Romeo's good at it though. Everything he says to Juliet is charming, flattering and considerate.

He Loses His Head a Lot — and Does Stupid Things

Romeo's very passionate — he's full of strong feelings. He rushes into whatever his feelings tell him to do.

1) The first time you see Romeo rushing into something is when he falls in love with Juliet. It happens instantly — and within 24 hours he's married to her. (Acts 1-2)

2) In Act 3, Tybalt kills Mercutio. Romeo's furious with himself that he let it happen, and furious with Tybalt. He kills Tybalt without stopping to think.

3) When Romeo hears Juliet's dead at the start of Act 5 he decides at once to go to Verona and poison himself.

Romeo's always rushing into things...

4) If Romeo slowed down and thought about what he was doing he wouldn't get into so much trouble.

He isn't Normally So Wet

You might think Romeo's a bit of a drip, but he isn't really being himself in a lot of the play.

In Act 2, Scene 4 Romeo's joking around with Mercutio and Benvolio. Mercutio is really relieved that Romeo's in a good mood:

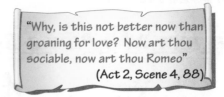

"Why, is this not better now than groaning for love? Now art thou sociable, now art thou Romeo"
(Act 2, Scene 4, 88)

The Romeo his friends know and love is a lot more fun than the one we get to see.

Romeo loses his head — he leaves it on the 37 bus...

There are loads of things to say about Romeo. These are just a few of the main points to get you started. Look out for other points about what Romeo's like as you read the play.

Juliet

You've got to know what Juliet's <u>really</u> like. Don't just assume that she's a <u>drippy girl</u>.

Juliet's a Capulet

The Capulets are another <u>wealthy</u> and <u>noble</u> Verona family — the Montagues' <u>enemies</u> in the feud.

I always get confused about who's from which <u>family</u>. This <u>rhyme</u>'s a great way to remember.

Juli-ET
Capul-ET

Juliet's only <u>thirteen</u> years old. She's definitely <u>not</u> a little girl — but she's young enough for some of the things that happen to be <u>mighty stressful</u>.

She's One Tough Cookie

When Juliet meets Romeo she falls in love with him <u>instantly</u> and <u>completely</u>.
From that moment the <u>most important</u> thing for Juliet is to be with Romeo, but it <u>isn't easy</u>:

1) The biggest problem is that he's a <u>Montague</u> — a deadly enemy of the Capulets.

2) Juliet's parents have got plans for her to <u>marry Paris</u>. The <u>last thing</u> they'll want to know is that she's in love with a Montague.

That's one tough cookie.

3) Romeo can go wandering around Verona at <u>any time</u> of day or night. Juliet's not even allowed out of the house in daytime without <u>permission</u>. She has to get the <u>Nurse</u> to organise her marriage <u>for her</u>.

4) In Act 3, Romeo kills <u>Tybalt</u> — Lady Capulet's nephew. That makes it even more <u>impossible</u> for Juliet to tell her parents about Romeo.

A Good Thing Too — She Has To Do Some Scary Things

Juliet can be <u>a bit soft</u> when she's with Romeo, but she does some <u>brave</u> things:

She risks cutting herself off from her <u>family</u>.

She takes a <u>sleeping potion</u> knowing she'll wake up in a <u>tomb</u>.
Act 4, Scene 3

She gets <u>married</u> in secret.
Act 2, Scene 6

She kills herself, because she'd rather be <u>dead</u> than alive <u>without</u> Romeo.
Act 5, Scene 3

<u>Some people</u> think Juliet's <u>immature</u> and gets <u>carried away</u> with love.
Maybe that's true, but you <u>can't</u> say the things she does are <u>easy</u>.

The diamond he swallowed — Jewel 'e 'et...

I don't think Juliet's all that wet, but some people think she <u>is</u>. Don't forget you can say <u>whatever you like</u> about her as long as you <u>back up</u> what you say with the words of the play.

Mercutio

I know it's a silly name, but Mercutio is probably the <u>coolest</u> character in the whole play.

Mercutio is a Bit of a *Star* and Romeo's *Best Mate*

Mercutio is Romeo's <u>best friend</u>.
He's bursting with <u>energy</u> and always
making jokes or <u>teasing</u> someone.
His speeches are full of <u>wordplay</u>, and <u>crazy ideas</u>.

He's Always *Taking The Mickey*

Mercutio calls Tybalt "*Prince of Cats*" and "*rat-catcher*" when he wants to wind him up.
He's got the name from a story called <u>*Reynard the Fox*</u> — it used to be very popular.
The <u>cat</u> character in the story was called <u>Tibalt</u>.

> Can't help thinking those luxury cracker party hats have gone to his head.

> Tybalt: What wouldst thou have with me?
> Mercutio: Good King of Cats, nothing but
>   one of your nine lives...
>   Act 3, Scene 1, 73-75

Even when Mercutio knows he's <u>dying</u> he still makes <u>jokes</u>:

> Ask for me tomorrow, and you shall find me a grave man.
>   Act 3, Scene 1, 92-93

"Grave" means "<u>serious</u>" and a place where you put <u>dead people</u> — geddit!

Mercutio's the *First Person to Die* in the Play

When Mercutio's killed it leaves a <u>big gap</u> in the <u>play</u>. All that <u>energy</u> suddenly <u>disappears</u>.
His death's really <u>sad</u> — it should <u>never</u> have happened.

1) Tybalt didn't want to fight <u>Mercutio</u>. Mercutio gets involved because Romeo looks <u>cowardly</u> when he won't fight Tybalt:

> O calm, dishonourable, vile submission!
>   Act 3, Scene 1, 70

Mercutio fights to protect Romeo's <u>honour</u>.

2) The fight is part of the <u>Montague-Capulet</u> feud. Mercutio isn't a member of <u>either</u> family. He blames the <u>feud</u> for his death:

> A plague a' both your houses!
> They have made worms' meat of me.
>   Act 3, Scene 1, 101-102

Worms meet.

3) He also blames <u>Romeo</u>. He only gets hurt when Romeo <u>gets in the way</u> trying to stop the fight.

Mercutio — doesn't that come before Venus...

The really important thing about Mercutio is he <u>fills up the stage</u> whenever he's on it with his nutty ideas and jokes. The jokes aren't all <u>side-splitters</u> but you can't say he doesn't try.

Tybalt & Benvolio

You've got to get these characters <u>clear</u> in your head — <u>strange names</u> and all.

Tybalt <u>is a</u> Troublemaker

Tybalt is Juliet's <u>cousin</u>, and Lady Capulet's <u>nephew</u>. He's always ready for a <u>fight</u>.
He fights Benvolio, Mercutio, <u>and</u> Romeo. He fights to defend the <u>honour</u> of the family.

This is what Tybalt says when he sees
Romeo in disguise at the <u>Capulet party</u>:

> Now, by the stock and honour of my kin
> To strike him dead I hold it not a sin.
> Act 1, Scene 5, 57-58

The <u>Capulets</u> Think Tybalt's Great...

Despite his <u>faults</u> the Capulets think Tybalt's <u>great</u>.
Juliet, her mum and the Nurse all say they're <u>sorry</u> about him dying.

> Nurse: O Tybalt, Tybalt, the best friend I ever had!
> O courteous Tybalt, honest gentleman,
> That ever I should live to see thee dead!
> Act 3, Scene 2, 61-3

Why do people say I'm a rubble maker?

...But He <u>Cheats</u> When He Fights Mercutio

Tybalt shows his <u>sneaky side</u> when he kills Mercutio. He stabs him <u>under Romeo's arm</u>.
Mercutio could have thought the fight was <u>over</u>, or not been able to <u>see</u> properly:

> [Tybalt under Romeo's arm thrusts Mercutio in.]
> Act 3, Scene 1, stage direction, line 85

Benvolio's <u>a</u> Nice Bloke — He Doesn't Get Killed

Benvolio is Romeo's <u>cousin</u>, and a <u>good friend</u>.
He tries to do the <u>right thing</u> and stay <u>out of trouble</u>.

> Part fools, you know not what you do.
> Act 1, Scene 1, 55-6

1) Benvolio always wants to <u>avoid fights</u>:

> I pray thee, good Mercutio, let's retire.
> The day is hot, the Capels are abroad,
> And if we meet we shall not scape a brawl.
> Act 3, Scene 1, 1-3

"abroad" means out and about, <u>not</u> out of the country.

2) Benvolio makes a <u>real effort</u> to cheer Romeo up when he's feeling down about Rosaline. He <u>persuades</u> him to go to the Capulets' party.

3) Benvolio tells Romeo to <u>run away</u> after he's killed Tybalt, and stays to <u>explain</u> what's happened to the Prince.

Shakespeare's cake files — Bun-folio...

Tybalt and Benvolio are <u>very different</u>. Benvolio tries to be <u>sweet</u>, and Tybalt is definitely a <u>pain</u>.
Start off by remembering the <u>basic points</u> about them and the other stuff should <u>follow on</u>.

Lord & Lady Montague

These are Romeo's mum and dad. Make sure you don't get them <u>muddled up</u> with Juliet's.

Montague *is Another* Nice Guy

Lord Montague is <u>Romeo</u>'s father.

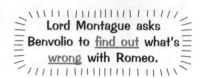

1) Lord Montague is the <u>head</u> of the Montague family.
   The Montagues are one of the <u>richest</u> and <u>most powerful</u> families in Verona.

2) Lord Montague <u>worries</u> about Romeo when he's unhappy:

> Could we but learn from whence his sorrows grow,
> We would as willingly give cure as know.
> Act 1, Scene 1, 145-6

Lord Montague asks Benvolio to <u>find out</u> what's <u>wrong</u> with Romeo.

3) At the end of the play Montague and Capulet agree to <u>give up</u> the feud. They make plans to put up <u>gold statues</u> in memory of their children.

4) When he patches up the quarrel with Capulet his wife and son are <u>both dead</u>. Montague is a <u>sad</u> figure at the end of the play.

Lady Montague *is a Real Sweetie*

Lady Montague is a <u>gentle</u> and <u>emotional</u> person.
She's very <u>concerned</u> about Romeo and her husband.

Lady Montague <u>restrains</u> Lord Montague from fighting at the beginning:

Lady Montague's my favourite character — she wouldn't hurt a fly...

> Lord Montague: Thou villain Capulet! — Hold me not, let me go.
> Lady Montague: Thou shalt not stir one foot to seek a foe.
> Act 1, Scene 1, 70-71

She literally <u>holds him back</u>.

She's <u>relieved</u> Romeo wasn't involved in the fighting:

> O, where is Romeo? Saw you him today?
> Right glad I am he was not at this fray.
> Act 1, Scene 1, 107-8

When Romeo's banished to Mantua it makes Lady Montague so unhappy she <u>dies of grief</u>.

...and concerned about his recent <u>unhappiness</u>.

Evolution in reverse — Man-ta-goo...

It's easy to think of the Montagues as goodies and the Capulets as baddies but it's <u>not</u> quite that simple. Don't forget the Montagues join in with the <u>feud</u> as happily as the Capulets do.

Lord & Lady Capulet

Time to find out about <u>Juliet's mum and dad</u>. Lord and Lady Capulet aren't such a lovely couple.

Capulet *Likes Getting His* Own Way

Lord Capulet's an <u>ambitious</u> man. He thinks he knows what's <u>best</u> for Juliet.

1) The Capulets are as <u>important</u> in Verona as the Montagues. Capulet wants to make them even more <u>influential</u>.

2) Paris is <u>rich</u>, <u>powerful</u> and related to the <u>Prince</u> — the ruler of Verona. That's why Capulet wants Juliet to get <u>married</u> to him.

3) Capulet thinks he knows what's best for Juliet. After Tybalt's death in Act 3 he rushes the wedding to Paris to cheer Juliet up — in fact it's the <u>last thing</u> she wants.

4) When Juliet says she won't marry Paris her father is so <u>angry</u> at her disobedience that he wants to hit her:

> My fingers itch.
> Act 3, Scene 5, 164

5) I wouldn't want Lord Capulet to be <u>my</u> dad, but you could say he tries his best. He's strict, but parents generally were <u>stricter</u> when Shakespeare wrote the play.

Lady Capulet *is an Ambitious Mum*

Lady Capulet's ambitious <u>too</u>. She's pretty <u>fierce</u> — especially with Juliet.

1) Lady Capulet sees all the <u>practical advantages</u> of Paris:

> So shall you share in all that he doth possess,
> By having him, making yourself no less.
> Act 1, Scene 3, 94-5

She's saying Juliet will get <u>wealth</u> and <u>status</u> by marrying Paris. She doesn't say anything about Juliet's <u>feelings</u> though.

2) When Juliet <u>doesn't</u> want to marry Paris, Lady Capulet says:

> I was your mother much upon these years
> That you are now a maid.
> Act 1, Scene 3, 73-74

Lady Capulet was <u>married</u> with a <u>baby</u> at Juliet's age. She thinks Juliet's being <u>childish</u> by refusing to get married.

3) Lady Capulet is <u>bloodthirsty</u>. She's quick to ask for Romeo's blood when he kills her <u>nephew</u> Tybalt.

Later she daydreams about hiring a man to <u>kill</u> Romeo:

> I'll send to one in Mantua,
> ...Shall give him such an unaccustomed dram
> That he shall soon keep Tybalt company.
> Act 3, Scene 5, 88, 90-91

Cap-u-let — hats for hire...

Remember if you say things like this in the test, you've got to <u>back up</u> your point with examples from the scene. That shows the examiner your points have come <u>from the play</u>.

Nurse

Right, this is where it gets a bit <u>weird</u>. Juliet's got a Nurse — only really she's more like a <u>nanny</u>.

The <u>Nurse</u> <u>is</u> <u>Not</u> There Because Juliet Is Sick

Let's get this clear <u>now</u> — the Nurse isn't a medical nurse. She's Juliet's nanny. She's <u>looked after</u> Juliet since she was a baby. She even did the breastfeeding. Lots of <u>rich families</u> employed nurses to <u>bring up</u> their children.

The Nurse Really <u>Loves</u> Juliet

The Nurse is a <u>comedy character</u> — she's a bit of an <u>old windbag</u>. She's very attached to Juliet, and does her best to help her.

1) The Nurse is more <u>affectionate</u> with Juliet than her mother ever is. She has <u>pet names</u> for her. In Act 1, Scene 3 she calls her a "lamb", a "ladybird", and a "pretty fool".

2) Juliet's a lot <u>closer</u> to the Nurse than she is to her mother because she's spent so much <u>time</u> with her.

3) When Juliet seems to be dead on the morning of the wedding to Paris the Nurse is more <u>genuinely upset</u> than any of the other characters.

She Helps Romeo and Juliet <u>Arrange Their Marriage</u>

The Nurse has <u>no choice</u> about helping Juliet marry Romeo. Juliet's the <u>boss</u> and she's the <u>servant</u>:

> I am a drudge, and toil in your delight.
> Act 2, Scene 5, 74

The Nurse probably thinks Juliet would be <u>better off</u> with Paris. When she's <u>under pressure</u> from her parents, the Nurse advises Juliet to <u>do as they say</u>:

> I think you are happy in this second match,
> For it excels your first.
> Act 3, Scene 5, 222-3

Juliet thinks the Nurse is being a <u>hypocrite</u>, but she's trying to be <u>practical</u> and <u>sensible</u>.

She's a Real <u>Gasbag</u> — She <u>Never</u> Gets to the Point

Once the Nurse starts talking it's really hard to <u>stop</u> her. She repeats herself <u>over and over</u> again:

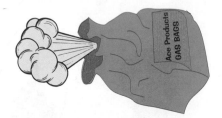

> O day, O day, O day, O hateful day!
> Never was seen so black a day as this.
> O woeful day, O woeful day!
> Act 4, Scene 5, 52-4

The Nurse is really <u>bad</u> at telling stories and passing on messages, because she takes so long to <u>get to the point</u>.

<u>Ow, it's sharp here — At last you've got to the point</u>

The Nurse can be a <u>right pain</u>, but she does her <u>best</u> for Juliet. She's also one of the <u>funnier</u> characters, so show the examiner <u>why</u> you think she's funny if she comes up in the test.

Friar Lawrence

Look out for this stuff when you write about the Friar...

The Friar Gives Advice to Romeo and Juliet

The Friar's <u>respected</u> for being an <u>educated</u> and <u>holy</u> man. He's <u>kind</u> and <u>sensible</u> but a bit <u>boring</u>.

1) A Friar is a sort of <u>monk</u>, who does some of the things parish priests do — he can perform <u>weddings</u> and <u>funerals</u>, and people go to see him with their <u>problems</u>.

2) Romeo and Juliet go to the Friar for <u>help</u> and <u>advice</u> when they can't get it from their parents — when Romeo wants to <u>marry</u> Juliet, and when Juliet wants to <u>get out of</u> marrying Paris.

3) The Friar's <u>good</u> at giving advice. He persuades Romeo not to kill himself in Act 3, Scene 3, and talks Juliet out of killing herself in Act 4, Scene 1.

The Nurse is <u>impressed</u> by the way he talks:

> O Lord I could have stay'd here all the night
> To hear good counsel. O what learning is!
> Act 3, Scene 3, 159-60

4) The Friar and the Nurse are the <u>only</u> people who know Romeo and Juliet's <u>secrets</u>.

The Friar Hopes The Wedding Will End The Feud

The Friar's <u>not</u> that keen to marry Romeo to Juliet.

He knows all about Romeo's crush on Rosaline, so he <u>can't believe</u> Romeo's serious about Juliet.

He helps because he hopes the wedding will <u>end the feud</u>:

> In one respect I'll thy assistant be;
> For this alliance may so happy prove
> To turn your households' rancor to pure love.
> Act 2, Scene 3, 90-92

But He Seems to Know Things Will Go Wrong

Even though the Friar's <u>hoping</u> the wedding will have happy results, he says lots of things that make it sound like he <u>knows</u> things will end up <u>going wrong</u>.

The advice he gives Romeo just before he gets married is particularly <u>spooky</u>:

> These violent delights have violent ends...
> Act 2, Scene 6, 9

One step closer and you'll feel <u>my</u> violent end!

The Friar's worried that Romeo's so <u>wrapped up</u> in his feelings he'll let things get completely <u>out of control</u>.

A large priest underwater — a deep fat friar...

In some ways Friar Lawrence is a bit like the Nurse — he <u>goes on</u> a bit, but tries to be helpful. Remember the stuff on this page, and you'll have a <u>head start</u> if the test asks about the Friar.

Paris, Prince & Others

Here's the last lot of characters to get to know, so get stuck in.

Paris Wants to Marry Juliet

Paris is conventional and polite to everyone.
He keeps his emotions hidden — you never know how he feels deep down.

1) Paris is a rich and influential nobleman. He's related to the Prince who rules Verona.

2) That makes him a useful ally for Capulet in city politics. If Paris marries Juliet he'll be family and have to help Capulet — that's why Capulet's so keen on the wedding.

3) In Act 5, Scene 3 you see Paris at Juliet's tomb. He says he'll bring flowers every night. It's a nice thing to say, but he doesn't let his feelings flood out the way Romeo does.

4) When Paris is dying he asks Romeo to put him in the tomb with Juliet. That shows a bit more emotion. He probably did love Juliet, just in a quieter, calmer way than Romeo.

Just Call Him Paris — Not Count or County

Paris's title is 'County'. A County is the same thing as a Count — a high-ranking nobleman. Shakespeare sometimes calls Paris 'Count' and sometimes 'County'.

It depends whether he wants a one or two syllable word to fit the rhythm of the line.

If I were you I'd just call him Paris — it gets confusing otherwise.

The Prince is the Police-Chief, Judge and Jury

The Prince rules Verona. He always turns up when there's been trouble or fighting to sort things out. He decides who gets punished and how.

There's something funny goin' on 'ere.

Even though he's really powerful he can't escape the violence of the feud. His relatives Paris and Mercutio both get killed:

> And I for winking at your discords too
> Have lost a brace of kinsmen.
> Act 5, Scene 3, 294-5

He speaks in really formal poetry — it makes him sound posher and more powerful.

Don't Worry About The Other Characters

There are two other characters you should just learn the names of — Balthasar is Romeo's servant, and Peter is the Nurse's servant.

There are lots of other characters in the play — musicians, servants, and townspeople. You can think of them like extras in a film. They're just there for a bit of padding — so ignore them and concentrate on the stars.

County Paris — is that Paris-shire perhaps...

More than one person to remember on this page. You don't need to know as much about them as about Romeo and Juliet, but you do need to know exactly who they are and what they do in the play.

Revision Summary

If you don't know who's who in the play it can get seriously confusing. You need to know the names of all the main characters — and how to spell them. What's more, you've got to know what they're like, and the main events they get involved in. Keep going through these questions, looking up ones you don't know, until you can answer them all without cheating. Answer them all, I said.

1) Who are the deadly enemies of the Montagues?
2) Is Romeo a Capulet or a Montague?
3) What does Romeo do that shows he can be dangerous?
4) Is Romeo calm, level-headed and in control of his feelings?
5) Is Juliet a complete drip?
6) Who do Juliet's parents want her to marry?
7) List three brave things Juliet does in the play.
8) Would you say Mercutio is a) a bit of a laugh, or b) dull as ditchwater?
9) Name Romeo's cousin and Juliet's cousin.
10) What are Mercutio's annoying nicknames for Tybalt?
11) What are two things Benvolio does to help Romeo?
12) Does Lord Montague worry about his son?
13) Why does Lady Montague die?
14) Why does Lord Capulet want Juliet to marry Paris?
15) Does Lady Capulet think Juliet should marry Paris?
16) What is the Nurse's job?
17) Does the Nurse love Juliet?
18) What does Friar Lawrence hope will be the result of Romeo and Juliet's marriage?
19) What does Paris ask Romeo to do when he's dying?
20) Who's the ruler of Verona?

I'd like to thank my momma and poppa. And I'd like to thank the Academy for their recognition of my achievements as a **CAR**-ACTOR.

ACT 1 SCENE 1	## What Happens in Act One

You have to write about <u>one</u> scene in the test and it could be <u>any scene</u>. This section tells the <u>story</u> of the play. It shows you clearly what <u>every scene's</u> about. Use it to learn the <u>whole story</u>.

Prologue — <u>The Whole Story In Fourteen Lines</u>

There's a feud going on in Verona
The Montagues and Capulets are two of Verona's noble families. The families quarrelled years ago and are still feuding. The story's about two lovers, one from each family. They will both die, but their deaths finally bring an end to the quarrel.
lines 1-14

The <u>quarrel</u> between the <u>Montagues and Capulets</u> affects <u>everything</u> that happens in the play and usually makes things <u>worse</u>.

<u>You know</u> right from the <u>start</u> of the play that Romeo and Juliet are going to <u>die</u>.

Scene One — <u>The First Big Fight; Romeo's Being Drippy</u>

The first big scene's got a <u>huge sword fight</u> — that's to make you sit up and pay attention.

You're so wet I could beat you with a spoon

①**A fight starts**
Servants of the Capulets start a fight with servants of the Montagues by insulting them. lines 1-56

②**Tybalt drags Benvolio in**
Benvolio tries to calm things down, but Tybalt forces him to fight. lines 57-63

③**It turns into a street brawl**
The fight turns into a general brawl. Lords Capulet and Montague and their wives arrive. lines 64-71

④**The Prince sorts it out**
The Prince stops the fighting and orders that the next person to cause trouble will be executed. lines 72-94

⑤**What's up with Romeo?**
Romeo's parents are worried about him. Benvolio promises to find out what's wrong. lines 95-146

⑥**He's in love and fed up**
Romeo tells Benvolio he is unhappy because he is in love with Rosaline, who doesn't love him. lines 151-229

Look out for Tybalt. Whenever he turns up in the play he causes <u>trouble</u>.

Calm it you lot...

Benvolio tells Romeo to <u>forget Rosaline</u> — there are plenty more fish in the sea.

Romeo's in love — with Rosaline. He <u>seems</u> dead serious about it.

The speech Romeo makes in lines 171-183 is full of <u>confusing opposites</u>:

> Feather of lead, bright smoke, cold fire, sick health, Still-waking sleep, that is not what it is.
> (171-2)

...he's saying love is cruel <u>as well as</u> kind because Rosaline won't love him back.

What Happens in Act One

It's no good <u>rushing</u> this section. In fact that's a <u>truly terrible</u> idea. The point is you could get <u>any</u> <u>scene</u> in the exam. Recognising <u>where</u> a scene comes in the story will be a <u>huge help</u> in the test.

Scene Two — Wedding **Plans and** Party **Plans**

1 Paris wants to marry Juliet
Capulet says that Paris can marry Juliet, but when she's a bit older, and only if she agrees. lines 1-33

2 Capulet's having a party
Capulet sends his servant to invite guests to the party that night. lines 34-43

3 Benvolio decides to gatecrash
Romeo and Benvolio speak to the servant and find out about the party. lines 44-81

4 Romeo's going too
Benvolio thinks a party will cure Romeo's love-sickness. lines 82-101

Paris is a relative of the Prince, the <u>ruler</u> of Verona. The wedding would give Capulet a <u>powerful</u>, <u>wealthy</u> ally in Verona.

Mercutio, Romeo's <u>best friend</u>, is invited to the party. He's another close relative of the Prince.

Come on misery-guts, let's gatecrash the party and meet some chicks.

Rosaline's invited too. Benvolio thinks the <u>beautiful</u> <u>girls</u> at the party will take Romeo's mind off her.

Scene Three — Juliet's Mother **Tells Her About Paris**

Juliet's mum and the Nurse think Paris is a real Mr Right — but Juliet's not so sure.

Let me tell you a story...blah, blah...

Yawn

Yawn

Juliet's mother thinks she's <u>old enough</u> to get married. Juliet's older than Lady Capulet was when she had Juliet.

Juliet says she will <u>try</u> to like Paris, but doesn't sound too <u>keen</u>:

I'll look to like, if looking liking move (98)

The Nurse tells the story about Juliet falling over <u>three times</u>. Once she gets an idea in her head she <u>harps on</u> until somebody tells her to <u>shut up</u>.

①**Juliet's mum wants a word**
Lady Capulet asks the Nurse to call Juliet. The Nurse tells a long-winded story about Juliet when she was a little girl, boring Lady Capulet and Juliet. lines 1-63

②**She tells Juliet about Paris**
Lady Capulet tells Juliet Paris wants to marry her. lines 64-100

③**They go to the party**
A servant comes to say Lady Capulet and Juliet are wanted at the party, and the Nurse is needed in the kitchen, and they all go. lines 101-106

What stage-hands do — they set the scene...

Swords and fights, a fair bit's happened already, and you're only on Scene 3. To <u>avoid</u> sounding <u>muddled</u> in the test you need to know the <u>order</u> things happen in. You <u>wouldn't</u> want to say something like Juliet's in love with Romeo before she's even met him, would you. That'd be <u>plain silly</u>.

ACT 1 SCENES 4 & 5 | *What Happens in Act One*

Remember you need to know <u>every scene</u> well enough to <u>recognise</u> it in the test.

Scene Four — *It's Party Time*

Romeo and Benvolio <u>shouldn't</u> be going to a Capulet party — only Mercutio's been invited.

All the guests are <u>wearing masks</u> — it's easy for Romeo and his friends to <u>sneak in</u> to their enemy's party.

There are lots of times in the play where Romeo gets warnings of terrible events through <u>dreams</u> or <u>visions</u>. This is the first.

Guess who?

① **Romeo's not in a party mood**
Mercutio, Benvolio and Romeo are about to go into Capulet's party. Romeo's friends are trying hard to cheer him up. lines 1-47

② **He's had a bad dream**
They are about to go in when Romeo mentions a dream he's had that makes him afraid to go to the party. lines 48-52

③ **Mercutio takes the mickey**
Mercutio describes nightly visits of the fairy, Queen Mab, to all sorts of people, and the dreams she makes them have. lines 53-103

④ **But Romeo's still worried**
Even after the teasing, Romeo can't relax, but they go on to the party. lines 104-114

Did the fairy mention that perhaps the 'R' on your top might blow the disguise?

There's a point to what Mercutio's saying — he's <u>teasing</u> Romeo for paying so much attention to his dreams.

Scene Five — **Romeo** <u>Annoys</u> **Tybalt** and <u>Charms</u> **Juliet**

① **The party's getting going**
The servants clear up after dinner, and Capulet encourages his guests to dance. lines 1-39

② **Romeo spots Juliet**
Romeo sees Juliet for the first time and thinks she's the most beautiful thing he's ever seen. lines 40-52

③ **Tybalt wants to fight him**
Tybalt spots Romeo, and wants to fight him. Lord Capulet tells him he can't. lines 53-91

④ **Romeo snogs Juliet**
Romeo goes up to Juliet and they begin to talk. They kiss, twice, and then the Nurse calls Juliet away. lines 92-110

⑤ **But their families are enemies**
Romeo doesn't know who Juliet is. He asks the Nurse and learns she's a Capulet. Juliet asks the Nurse who Romeo is and finds out he's a Montague. lines 111-143

Phoarrrrrr She's a babe!

ROMEO'S MASK

...but who's that guy with the big nose?

It was only three scenes ago that Romeo said he was in love with <u>Rosaline</u>.

Uh-oh, it's Tybalt. He <u>obeys</u> Capulet here, but the next day he sends a <u>letter</u> to Romeo challenging him to a <u>duel</u>.

Lines 93-106 are a <u>sonnet</u> (see P.26). Romeo and Juliet understand each other so well that even their first conversation is a <u>love poem</u>. By the end of the sonnet they are <u>in love</u> and they kiss.

Juliet won't marry Paris — she's in love with Rome-o

Act 1's fairly plain sailing, so there's no excuse for not <u>learning the story</u> so far really well. <u>Scribble down</u> the main event from each scene of Act 1 and <u>learn them</u> before you hit Act 2.

Section Five — Understanding the Story

What Happens In Act Two

**ACT 2
SCENES 1 & 2**

You've met all the main characters and it's time for the story to really take off. This act's a bit more lovey-dovey. It's got that famous balcony scene. More fights to come in Act 3.

Chorus — Time for a Recap

The story so far...
Romeo's forgotten Rosaline. Juliet's as much in love with Romeo as he is with her. They'll find it hard to meet. lines 144-157

Scene One — Mercutio and Benvolio Call it a Night

Don't forget the feud — it's dangerous for Romeo to be in the Capulets' garden.

① **Romeo wants to find Juliet**
Romeo breaks into the Capulets' garden looking for Juliet. lines 1-2

② **His friends leave him to it**
Mercutio and Benvolio look for Romeo, but can't find him and go home. lines 3-42

Not surprising really — it's almost dawn.

Scene Two — It's That Slushy Balcony Scene...Yuck

This scene's tense and rushed. Romeo and Juliet could get caught at any minute.

① **Romeo overhears Juliet**
Juliet comes out onto her balcony, not knowing Romeo's down below. lines 1-32

② **She's talking to herself**
Juliet wishes Romeo wasn't a Montague, or that she wasn't a Capulet — because she loves him. lines 33-49

③ **Romeo speaks to her**
Juliet recognises Romeo and almost her first thought is that he's in danger. lines 49-84

④ **Juliet's a bit embarrassed**
Romeo's heard her say how much she loves him but she won't take it back because it's true. lines 85-106

⑤ **Romeo says he loves her**
Romeo tries to swear he loves her too, but Juliet feels everything is too rushed. The Nurse is calling her, and she goes inside. lines 107-141

⑥ **They talk about getting married**
Juliet comes back and suggests they get married. He promises to decide by the next day. They say goodnight and Juliet goes in. lines 142-189

Juliet's saying Romeo should stop being a Montague, or she should stop being a Capulet. That way they can be together:

> O Romeo, Romeo, wherefore art thou Romeo?
> Deny thy father and refuse thy name;
> Or, if thou wilt not, be but sworn my love,
> And I'll no longer be a Capulet.
>
> (33-36)

Eh up pet, you look right nice!

You're not so bad yourself chuck.

He watched a football trick — ball-con-e-seen...

OK, so this bit gets a bit mushy — but it's really famous mushy scene. So it's dead important you understand what's going on. Romeo and Juliet are really loved up and they've already decided to marry.

ACT 2 SCENES 3 & 4	# What Happens in Act Two

The <u>cat's</u> out of the <u>bag</u>. Romeo <u>loves</u> Juliet and Juliet <u>loves</u> Romeo. We all know it's going to <u>end in tears</u>, so if I were you I'd enjoy the happy bits while they last. And <u>learn</u> the story.

Scene Three — Romeo Books the Church

That means it's <u>not long</u> after Romeo said goodbye to Juliet.

Keep up, Rosaline's old news. I'm madly in love with Juliet now.

Herbaceous dude!

① **Friar Lawrence rants about herbs**
It's dawn on the morning after the party. Friar Lawrence is setting out to gather medicinal plants. He says that plants used to cure can be misused to kill. lines 1-30

② **Romeo comes for a chat**
Romeo arrives. Friar Lawrence is surprised to see him up so early. He guesses Romeo hasn't been to bed at all. The Friar thinks Romeo has been with Rosaline. lines 31-44

③ **He says he's in love with Juliet now**
Romeo explains that he's completely forgotten Rosaline and wants to marry Juliet. lines 45-64

④ **The Friar will help them get married**
Friar Lawrence is amazed how quickly Romeo's fallen in love again. Romeo says this is completely different because Juliet loves him back. The Friar reluctantly agrees to the wedding. lines 65-94

Scene Four — The Nurse Takes a Bit of Stick

It's dangerous for Romeo and Juliet to meet in <u>public</u>. That's why the Nurse has to be their <u>messenger</u>.

① **Tybalt wants to fight Romeo**
Mercutio and Benvolio are talking about Tybalt's challenge to Romeo. lines 1-31

② **Romeo's a lot happier this morning**
Romeo appears and Mercutio and Benvolio joke and fool around with him. lines 32-81

③ **Juliet's Nurse comes to see Romeo**
The Nurse arrives as Juliet's messenger, with her servant Peter. The boys think she's really funny and tease her. Benvolio and Mercutio leave. lines 82-120

④ **He tells her when the wedding is**
The Nurse is upset by the teasing. Romeo tells her the wedding will be that afternoon. lines 121-181

A "challenge" means a <u>dare</u> to fight a <u>duel</u>. Romeo will look like a <u>coward</u> if he doesn't fight Tybalt.

This is the first time Romeo's friends have seen him <u>cheerful</u> since the beginning of the play.

The Nurse is trying hard to be <u>posh</u> and taking herself a bit too <u>seriously</u>.

Wedding this afternoon.

Woof!

No hurry — Romeo wasn't built in a day you know...

I'm not just being a <u>boring nag</u> you know — you really do need to <u>learn the story</u>. The important thing is to remember roughly <u>what</u> happens in each scene, and the <u>order</u> it happens in.

What Happens In Act Two

Two more scenes to go in this act, so make sure you get 'em <u>read and remembered</u>. The <u>clearer</u> you've got the play in your head the <u>easier</u> it'll be to write about the scene you get in the test.

Scene Five — Good News For Juliet

① **Juliet's in a bit of a tizz**
She's waiting impatiently for the Nurse.
lines 1-17

② **The Nurse brings the good news**
The Nurse arrives. She won't give Romeo's answer straight away and pretends she's exhausted from running the errand. Finally she tells Juliet that Romeo will marry her, and the wedding will be that afternoon. lines 18-77

The Nurse really <u>enjoys</u> being so important and being the <u>centre of attention</u>. That's why she <u>drags out</u> giving Juliet the message for so long.

There are no big preparations for the wedding. It's all got to be done in <u>secret</u>.

Scene Six — Get Your Confetti Out

The cell is where the Friar <u>lives</u>, — <u>not</u> a prison cell.

① **The Friar gives some advice**
Romeo is waiting at the Friar's cell. Friar Lawrence says he hopes nothing bad will come of the wedding. Romeo says he doesn't care, because there is enough happiness in just a minute spent with Juliet. The Friar warns Romeo not to be so extreme — if he is a bit calmer his happiness will last longer. lines 1-15

② **Here comes the bride**
Juliet arrives and all three set off for the church. lines 16-37

Holy smoke — the deep fat Friar's gone up in flames

Act 2 is the <u>happiest</u> part of the play, but there are still hints of <u>trouble</u> to come. In Scene 4 we find out Tybalt has challenged Romeo to a duel. There's no escaping that miserable feud. <u>Scribble down</u> the main events from Act Two from <u>here</u> and then from <u>memory</u>.

**ACT 3
SCENE 1**

What Happens in Act Three

Well, I said there'd be fighting and here it is. Act Three is a real mixture of happy and sad bits. Mainly though it's where things start going seriously wrong for Juliet and Romeo.

Scene One — Two Deadly Swordfights

There's lots of action in this scene — it's tricky to follow so take it chunk by chunk.

① **Benvolio's scared**
Mercutio and Benvolio are out in the street. Benvolio thinks they should go home. Mercutio refuses and starts making jokes about Benvolio, saying he's a trouble-maker. lines 1-31

Benvolio isn't really the sort of person who starts fights, but Mercutio enjoys pretending he is.

You alright back there Mercutio?.... Mercutio?....

② **Tybalt comes looking for Romeo**
Tybalt appears. He wants to fight Romeo but Mercutio starts teasing him. lines 32-52

③ **Romeo arrives but he won't fight**
Tybalt tries to make Romeo fight but he won't. No one can understand why. Mercutio steps in. lines 53-71

Romeo won't fight because Tybalt is Juliet's cousin. He doesn't want to kill a relative.

④ **Mercutio will**
Mercutio and Tybalt fight. Romeo tries to stop the fight by stepping between them. lines 72-85

Mercutio and Tybalt don't know about the wedding. They think Romeo's being a coward.

⑤ **Tybalt stabs Mercutio**
Tybalt gets a thrust under Romeo's arm and wounds Mercutio, then runs away. line 85

Mercutio is really angry with Romeo for getting in the way.

*A plague a' both your houses!
They have made worms' meat of me*
(101-102)

Mercutio curses both the Capulets and the Montagues. Their feud has killed him.

⑥ **Mercutio dies**
Mercutio is badly wounded. His page goes for a doctor. Benvolio helps him to a nearby house. Moments later Benvolio returns – Mercutio is dead. lines 85-113

⑦ **Romeo kills Tybalt**
Romeo is furious and upset. When Tybalt comes back Romeo is ready to fight. He kills Tybalt and runs off. lines 114-131

⑧ **Romeo's in big trouble now**
The Prince and Lord and Lady Capulet and Montague arrive to find out what's been going on. Benvolio explains. The Prince banishes Romeo from Verona. lines 132-192

Lovely motor, low mileage, one careful lady Verona...

This scene's just bursting with important events. Mercutio dies, Tybalt dies, and Romeo gets banished to Mantua. It's no good just knowing those things happened — you've got to know the order they happened in too. Scribble down a quick list for this scene and learn it.

What Happens in Act Three

Scene Two — Bad News for Juliet

In this scene Juliet gets so <u>upset</u> and <u>confused</u> she talks more to <u>herself</u> than she does to the Nurse.

① **Juliet can't wait for evening**
Juliet is happy and excited. She wants night to fall so Romeo can visit her. lines 1-31

<u>We know</u> Tybalt's dead and Romeo's banished, but Juliet doesn't. She's happy now but it <u>won't last</u>.

② **The Nurse says Romeo's killed Tybalt**
The Nurse comes in very upset because someone's died. Juliet thinks Romeo's dead. At last the Nurse explains it's Tybalt. lines 32-72

Juliet is <u>worried</u> as soon as she sees the Nurse. By taking so long to explain, the Nurse gets her into <u>even more</u> of a state.

③ **Juliet can't believe it**
At first Juliet's shocked that Romeo could do something so evil. lines 73-84

④ **The Nurse criticises Romeo**
The Nurse agrees with Juliet that Romeo's done a terrible thing. Juliet gets angry with the Nurse for blaming Romeo. lines 85-97

⑤ **Juliet makes excuses for Romeo**
Tybalt would have killed Romeo so Romeo was right to kill him. lines 98-109

Hysterical

⑥ **She thinks she won't see him again**
Now Juliet thinks about the fact Romeo's been banished and becomes hysterical. The Nurse goes to fetch Romeo. lines 110-143

Juliet's so unhappy at the end of the scene she says she wants to <u>die</u>.

Scene Three — Romeo's In A Real Mess

You could get <u>this very scene</u> in the test. You could get <u>any</u> of them. So read them <u>all</u>.

Romeo's hiding in the Friar's cell because he's <u>safe</u> from arrest there — it's a '<u>sanctuary</u>'.

It's no good I'm going to end it all.

Get over it you big Jessie!

Romeo's as <u>upset</u> as Juliet was in Scene 2.

① **The Friar tells Romeo he's banished**
Romeo's at Friar Lawrence's cell. The Friar comes to tell him he's banished. Romeo says that's worse than death. lines 1-70

② **Romeo says he'll kill himself**
When the Nurse arrives Romeo is ashamed he's killed Juliet's cousin. He threatens to kill himself. lines 71-108

③ **Friar Lawrence talks him out of it**
The Friar convinces Romeo that killing himself is pointless. He tells him to say goodbye to Juliet, then go to Mantua. lines 108-158

④ **Romeo goes to see Juliet**
Romeo leaves, happy and excited about seeing Juliet. lines 159-175

The Friar's advice is all <u>common sense</u>. Romeo should behave like a man, and be pleased — he's alive, Juliet's alive, he was banished not executed, and Tybalt, his enemy, is dead.

Romeo's fallen in his dinner — He's in a meal mess...

Everything's getting <u>messy</u> — Juliet is upset cos Romeo has killed Tybalt. Romeo's <u>upset</u> cos he thinks he's ruined everything. Remember <u>what</u> they're upset about, and what they <u>decide</u> to do.

| ACT 3 SCENES 4 & 5 | # What Happens in Act Three |

It strikes me this story is getting <u>mighty tricky</u>. It's <u>not worth</u> getting in a muddle.
Skim back through this section to <u>check</u> the bits you're not clear about <u>before</u> you read on.

Scene Four — *The Capulets and Paris Set a Date*

Such a fine suitor for our darling daughter. I let him drink the last can of fizzy orange.

Oh so the last Tango's in Paris.

Juliet's father has decided to get her <u>married off</u> as quickly as possible.

Capulet says Paris can marry Juliet
Lord and Lady Capulet are talking to Paris about his marriage to Juliet. Capulet promises that Juliet will marry him in three days' time. lines 1-35

Scene Five — *Seriously Bad News for Juliet*

For all Romeo and Juliet know at this point everything's going to be <u>all right</u>.

① **Romeo and Juliet say goodbye**
Early next day Romeo leaves Juliet for Mantua. They drag out saying goodbye, but eventually Romeo has to go. lines 1-59

② **Juliet's mum comes to see her**
Lady Capulet comes in and finds Juliet crying. She thinks Juliet's crying for Tybalt. She also thinks Juliet's upset because Romeo wasn't executed. Juliet has to play along with this. lines 60-103

③ **She says Juliet's got to marry Paris**
To cheer Juliet up Lady Capulet tells her about the marriage to Paris. Juliet says she won't marry Paris — that she would rather marry Romeo. lines 104-125

④ **Juliet's dad says he'll force her**
Lord Capulet arrives and tells Juliet to pull herself together. He quickly loses patience. Both Juliet's parents are furious and leave. lines 126-195

⑤ **The Nurse tells Juliet to marry Paris**
Juliet asks for the Nurse's help, but she sides with Juliet's parents. Juliet's furious and decides to see the Friar. If she has no better option she'll kill herself. lines 196-242

There's a voice, keeps on calling me, down the road, that's where I'll always be...

Mantua
Verona

Juliet can't marry Paris — she's <u>already married</u>. If she gets married again she'll be <u>breaking</u> the city's laws and Church <u>law</u>.

Lord Capulet is <u>really harsh</u> in this scene. He tells Juliet he will throw her out if she doesn't marry Paris.

Lady Capulet isn't as cross, she just thinks Juliet is being <u>stupid</u> to refuse such a good marriage.

Juliet's having a terrible time and not even the <u>Nurse</u> will support her.

Rooooooarrrrrrrrrrrrrrrrrrr

Baseball Capulets — *medieval American headgear...*

Romeo's best friend's <u>dead</u>. Romeo and Juliet are married but <u>can't</u> be together for more than a night. Juliet's being made to <u>marry</u> someone she doesn't even know. Not a very cheerful act really. <u>Learn</u> all the <u>main events</u> — it's sad stuff, but you've got to know it to <u>do well</u> in your test.

What Happens in Act Four

Act Four's <u>not</u> even slightly <u>happy</u>, but the story's <u>not hard</u> to follow — Juliet's parents are <u>frantic</u> to get her married to Paris and Juliet does <u>everything</u> she can to get out of it.

Scene One — Friar Lawrence's Cunning Plan

① **Paris is arranging his wedding**
Paris is talking to the Friar. lines 1-17

② **Juliet arrives as Paris is leaving**
She's polite but distant. He tries to be friendly. lines 18-43

③ **Juliet won't marry Paris**
Juliet tells the Friar she would rather kill herself than marry Paris. lines 44-67

④ **The Friar's got a plan**
Friar Lawrence sees she's deadly serious and makes a plan. Juliet will take a sleeping potion that makes her look dead. After she's buried Romeo will come and rescue her. Juliet agrees to the plan. lines 68-126

Paris says Capulet arranged the wedding to <u>cheer Juliet up</u>.

Friar Lawrence is in a <u>tricky position</u>. He can't let Juliet get married twice, and he can't let on about Romeo and Juliet.

Paris <u>thinks</u> Juliet wants to marry him.

After being <u>cold and polite</u> with Paris, Juliet gets very emotional and shows her <u>real feelings</u>.

Do you know you're the spitting image of Yoda?

Scene Two — Juliet Plays the Dutiful Daughter

This is one of the shortest scenes in the play — but that doesn't mean it's not <u>important</u>.

① **Capulet's organising the wedding**
The Capulet household is preparing for the wedding. lines 1-13

② **Juliet agrees to marry Paris**
Juliet comes back from the Friar's. She tells her parents she's sorry she was disobedient and that she'll marry Paris. lines 14-46

The wedding's going ahead even though Juliet has <u>never agreed</u> to marry Paris.

If course I'll marry Paris... .....not.

Scene Three — A Spoonful of Sugar...

① **Juliet has an early night**
Juliet's Nurse and mother want to help her get ready for the wedding, but Juliet says she needs to sleep and says good night. lines 1-13

② **She takes the sleeping potion**
Juliet gets ready to take the Friar's potion. At first she's afraid it won't work, then worries it'll kill her, or that she'll go mad when she wakes up in the tomb. She imagines she sees Tybalt's ghost kill Romeo, then drinks the potion. lines 14-58

She's got a <u>dagger</u> just in case.

It's like Romeo's dreams, a <u>warning</u> of what will happen later on.

Scottish jokers — I thought you said punning clan...

The Friar is helping Juliet out of a <u>sticky situation</u> here — but it's a <u>risky plan</u> too. It's pretty <u>brave</u> of Juliet to take a potion that might kill her. I guess some people will do anything for love.

| Act 4 Scenes 4 & 5 | # What Happens in Act Four |

Everything's still going according to the Friar's plan. If you get a scene from this bit of the play in the test you need to know the plan and who's in on it and who's not.

Scene Four — Capulet's in a Fluster

It's almost time for the wedding
Capulet, Lady Capulet and the Nurse are in a flurry preparing the house for Juliet and Paris's wedding. lines 1-28

While Juliet's parents are preparing for the wedding, Juliet is doing her best to make sure it won't happen.

Scene Five — It's All So Terribly Sad

On the surface this scene looks really sad, but the way the Nurse and the Capulets carry on makes it quite funny. A good thing too because the next act's miserable.

①**The Nurse thinks Juliet's dead**
The Nurse thinks Juliet is sleeping late, then believes that she's dead. lines 1-16

We know Juliet's going to look dead, but it's the last thing her parents and Nurse expect to see.

②**Juliet's parents hear the news**
Lady Capulet comes to Juliet's room, and the Nurse tells her Juliet's dead. lines 17-21

③**Everyone gets very upset**
Lord Capulet, Friar Lawrence and Paris arrive for the wedding with a band of musicians. Paris, the Nurse and Juliet's parents are all very upset. lines 22-64

The Nurse is probably more upset than anyone — the trouble is she repeats herself so much she starts to sound daft.

④**The Friar calms them all down**
He takes control of the situation and gets preparations for the funeral under way. lines 65-95

⑤**The wedding turns into a funeral**
Everyone but the Nurse and the musicians leaves. Peter comes in and tries to get the musicians to play something cheerful. They refuse. Peter insults them, but the musicians win the argument and they all leave. lines 96-138

Unfortunately Juliet snuffed it last night so the wedding's off. Funeral later today.

This bit with the musicians is quite strange, and not very funny. It could be there to give the audience a rest after all the moaning and wailing.

Poison — that's what they think Julie-ate...

This might seem like a fussy point but I promise you it's dead important. You've got to learn who knows what as well as who does what — like the Friar knowing Juliet's not really dead but her parents and the Nurse having no idea. It helps explain why people do what they do, and if you know that you'll be able to write stacks better in the test.

What Happens in Act Five

The last act! You're a mole's whisker away from knowing the story top to bottom — that could save your bacon in the Shakespeare test. Don't start rushing just because it's the last act.

Scene One — Romeo Gets the Wrong End of the Stick

There's still a tiny chance things will turn out OK for Romeo and Juliet, but just about everything that could go wrong in Act Five does.

As usual Romeo pays attention to his dreams. He's right to imagine Juliet will kiss him when he's dead, but wrong to think she'll be able to bring him back to life.

Off to Verona on a badly drawn horse

Romeo still doesn't know about the Friar's plan, so he thinks Juliet really is dead.

An apothecary is somebody who knows how to make medicines. It's an old name for a chemist.

① **Romeo's had a good dream**
Romeo is in Mantua. He has dreamt that he was dead, and that Juliet brought him back to life with a kiss. He believes this is a good sign. lines 1-11

② **But he hears that Juliet's dead**
Balthasar, Romeo's servant, arrives from Verona and tells Romeo Juliet is dead. Romeo sends Balthasar to organise horses so they can go back to Verona. lines 12-33

③ **Romeo decides to go to her tomb**
Romeo plans to return to Verona and kill himself in Juliet's tomb. lines 34-57

④ **He buys some poison to kill himself**
Romeo calls on an apothecary, and asks for lethal poison. The apothecary doesn't want to sell it because it's illegal, but he really needs the money, so he lets Romeo have it. lines 57-86

Scene Two — The Friar's Letter Didn't Get Through

Here's the first thing to go wrong.

The Friar's message never got through
Friar John, Friar Lawrence's messenger to Romeo, comes back from Mantua. He couldn't deliver the letter explaining the Friar's plan. Friar Lawrence decides to be at the Capulet tomb when Juliet wakes up, and to write to Romeo again. lines 1-30

Ahhh, don't shoot the messenger.

Uh-oh — the Friar doesn't think Romeo will have heard about Juliet's death. He doesn't know how urgent it is to find Romeo and tell him what's really going on.

No friar's letter — so the friar's let'er die?

You must know what I'm going to say by now. Learning the story really helps you. It's not that you've got to know every little detail, but just be able to recognise the scene you get in the test.

ACT 5 SCENE 3 | What Happens in Act Five

This is it, the last scene of the last act. There are only three scenes in Act 5, but to make up for it Scene 3's a whopper. It's full of misunderstandings and deaths — a proper tragedy.

Scene Three — Till Death Do Us Part

Another action-packed scene — now with bonus slushy bits.

① **Paris visits Juliet's grave**
Paris comes to the tomb to say goodbye to Juliet. He says he will come to the tomb every night to lay flowers and mourn. lines 1-17

② **Romeo arrives**
Romeo and Balthasar arrive. Warned by his page, Paris steps away from the tomb so he can watch them. lines 18-21

③ **He sends his servant away**
Romeo gives Balthasar a letter for his father. Romeo tells Balthasar that he will kill him if he follows him into the tomb. lines 22-42

④ **Secretly the servant stays**
Balthasar stays nearby, worried about Romeo's state of mind. lines 43-44

⑤ **Romeo opens the tomb**
Romeo starts opening up the entrance to the tomb. Paris sees him. He thinks Romeo's going to vandalise the tomb and knows he's meant to be banished from Verona. lines 45-53

Romeo has come to prove his love for Juliet. He's come to the tomb to die beside her.

Romeo is tense and desperate.

Paris thinks it's Romeo's fault that Juliet is dead. He thinks she died of grief for Tybalt.

This tomb malarkey is putting us gravediggers out of business.

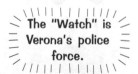

The "Watch" is Verona's police force.

Romeo never planned to kill Paris. Paris just gets in the way of his plan to die with Juliet.

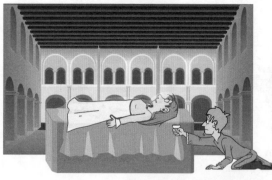

Romeo doesn't hate Paris, because they've both had to suffer Juliet's supposed death.

Romeo's in a terrible hurry. If he waited five minutes, and was alive when Juliet woke up, everything would work out fine.

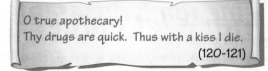

O true apothecary!
Thy drugs are quick. Thus with a kiss I die.
(120-121)

⑥ **Paris tries to arrest him**
Paris threatens to arrest Romeo. Romeo doesn't recognise him and begs him to go away. lines 54-70

⑦ **Romeo kills Paris**
They fight. Paris's page runs off to fetch the Watch. Romeo gives Paris a fatal wound. As he dies he asks to be buried alongside Juliet. Romeo agrees. lines 71-74

⑧ **Romeo puts Paris in the tomb**
Now Romeo recognises Paris and puts him in the tomb. lines 74-87

⑨ **Romeo kills himself**
Romeo is amazed that Juliet still looks so fresh and alive. He takes his poison and dies. lines 88-120

What Happens in Act Five

Crumbs, this scene is <u>huge</u>, and pretty complicated too.
Take it one <u>bite-sized chunk</u> at a time and you'll find it <u>easier to swallow</u>.

Hope You've Got Your <u>Hanky</u>

The Friar's <u>afraid</u> of being caught by the Watch with Romeo and Paris's <u>bodies</u>. If he was less timid here he could <u>stop</u> Juliet from killing herself.

Ooh! That's a bit tickly

The Watch would <u>stop</u> Juliet from killing herself if they found her.

Nobody seems very surprised that Juliet's <u>died twice</u>.

Lady Montague <u>died</u> in the night, because she was so <u>sad</u> about Romeo's exile.

⑩ Friar Lawrence arrives
The Friar arrives ready to open the tomb. Balthasar comes out of his hiding place and explains that Romeo is already inside. lines 121-143

⑪ He sees the bodies
Friar Lawrence goes into the tomb and sees Paris and Romeo dead. lines 144-146

⑫ He tells Juliet to leave
Juliet wakes up. The Friar realises the plan's gone wrong and wants Juliet to come away from the tomb. She won't leave and he runs. lines 147-159

⑬ Juliet kills herself too
Juliet tries to take poison from Romeo's lips. She hears the Watch coming, and stabs herself with Romeo's dagger. lines 160-170

⑭ Everyone's very confused
The Watch arrive with Paris's Page, and send for the Prince. He quickly arrives, followed by Lord and Lady Capulet. The Watch explain that Paris and Romeo are dead, and Juliet is dead again. lines 171-207

⑮ The Prince gets to the bottom of the story
Montague arrives. The Prince tells him Romeo is dead. The Prince asks for an explanation of what's happened. The Friar tells his part of the story. Balthasar hands over Romeo's letter, which backs up the Friar's story. lines 208-290

⑯ The End
The Prince tells Capulet and Montague that their feud has killed Romeo, Juliet, Mercutio and Paris. Capulet and Montague make peace, and agree to put up gold statues in memory of their children. The Prince asks everyone to leave. lines 291-310

Friar Lawrence says he should be <u>executed</u> if anything is his fault. But he makes everything sound like a big accident so he can't be blamed.

Phew!

I'd shake hands if I could change my posture

Go hence, to have more talk of these sad things;
Some shall be pardon'd and some punished:
For never was a story of more woe
Than this of Juliet and her Romeo.

(307-310)

Sniff, sigh — this story makes me tomb miserable...

That's it then, the complete story of <u>*Romeo and Juliet*</u>. The only way to be <u>sure</u> you know it is to test whether you can tell the story <u>off by heart</u>. You <u>don't</u> need to memorise it scene by scene, but if you've got a <u>perfect picture</u> of events in <u>each act</u> the test'll be a <u>breeze</u>.

Revision Summary

Blimey — I never knew <u>Romeo and Juliet</u> was so long. That's why it's important to get this section clear. In your SAT you'll only get one scene — but you'll do much better if you know where it comes in the story. Think about it — you don't want to be writing about things that happen later in the play as if they've already happened. The examiners will think you don't know what you're talking about. Just get the story clear and you can save all this bother.

Try these revision questions — see if you can work through all of them without looking back over the section.

1) What does the prologue tell us about Romeo and Juliet right at the start?

2) Who stops the fighting in Act 1 Scene 1?

3) Who is Romeo in love with in Act 1 Scene 1?

4) Who wants to marry Juliet in Act 1 Scene 2?

5) Why does Benvolio decide they should go to the Capulets' party in Act 1 Scene 2?

6) How do Romeo and Benvolio sneak into the party in Act 1 Scene 4?

7) In which scene do Romeo and Juliet meet for the first time?

8) Why is Act 2 Scene 2 so tense?

9) Who does Romeo go to see to organise his wedding?

10) In which act and scene does the Nurse come to arrange the wedding?

11) In which act and scene does Juliet find out she's getting married to Romeo?

12) Who gets killed in Act 3 Scene 1?

13) What happens to Romeo at the end of Act 3 Scene 1?

14) What emotion does Juliet feel at the end of Act 3 Scene 2?

15) What does Romeo threaten to do in Act 3 Scene 3?

16) In which scene do Capulet and Paris set a date for Paris's wedding to Juliet?

17) What does Capulet say he will do if Juliet refuses to marry Paris in Act 3 Scene 5?

18) In which act and scene does Juliet take the sleeping potion?

19) In which act and scene does the nurse find Juliet and think she's dead?

20) In which act and scene do Romeo and Juliet die?

That's gotta be bard for you!

Writing About Characters

This is the easiest kind of task you can get asked to do in the SAT — you have to write about one of the characters in the scene. It's pretty straightforward — as long as you get this method clear.

Writing About Characters Isn't That Tricky

Here's a typical task about a character — remember, it'll probably look really hard at first.

This is where you've got to look. →

Romeo and Juliet

Act 3 scene 5, line 37 to the end of the scene

TASK 1

In this scene, Juliet's parents insist she must marry Paris.

What problems does Juliet face, and how does she react to them in this scene?

The bit in **bold** is the actual task.

You've got to write about what happens to Juliet in the scene, and how she reacts — what she does and says.

I wouldn't blame you for thinking: "How am I supposed to know what Juliet's problems are? I don't know what's going on inside her head." The thing is, you can work it all out from the bit of the play you get. It's not as hard as it looks — there are plenty of clues.

These clues are dead helpful. They tell you what to write about.

Remember, you have to write about all four of these things. If you don't, you'll lose a whole load of marks.

Before you begin to write you should think about:

- Juliet's worries as she speaks to her mother.
- The confrontation between Juliet and her father.
- The Nurse's advice, and Juliet's reaction.
- Juliet's situation at the end of the scene.

What a friendly, appealing character!

Careful — There are Two Bits to This Question

This question is about what happens AND Juliet's reaction.
'How Juliet reacts' means these three things — look out for them:

1) What she says — and how she says it.
2) What she doesn't say — she doesn't mention Romeo to her father at all.
3) What she does — she gets down on her knees to beg her father to listen to her.

Sometimes the clues are in the stage directions, sometimes they're in the words.

Follow the Method

There's a lot to think about, so it's a good idea to do it one step at a time.

It's Not Hard if You Follow This Method

This kind of question is boring — that's the bad news. The good news is that it's nice and straightforward. The key is to make totally sure that you answer each of the points.

The best way to do this is to take a step-by-step approach.

1) Go through each of the points they give you one by one.
2) Look at the scene, find the bits that tell you something about that point and make notes.
3) Your answer should be made up of all the things you've noticed.

OK — Start with the First Point...

> Juliet's worries as she speaks to her mother.

This is all you have to think about for now.

You've got to work out what Juliet's worries are. Look at the bit of the scene just before Lady Capulet arrives — that tells you what Juliet's doing before the conversation with her mother.

(1) *In the very first bit, Juliet says goodbye to Romeo — she doesn't know if she'll see him again.*

> JULIET   O, think'st thou we shall ever meet again?

_ So at the start of the scene Juliet's worried about Romeo — that's one of her worries.

WINTER SPORTS
Hedgehog Bombarding in Pencil-vania

Get your prey in your sights
— aim
— start with the first point, then totally cover the swine...

(2) *When her mother comes in, she finds Juliet crying. She thinks Juliet's upset about Tybalt's death.*

> LADY CAPULET: Evermore weeping for your cousin's death?

We know Juliet's actually upset about Romeo leaving. Romeo was banished because he killed Tybalt — so Lady Capulet starts slagging him off. She calls him a "traitor murderer".

Juliet's parents hate Romeo — that's another worry.

(3) *Then Lady Capulet tells Juliet she's going to be married to Paris.*

> The County Paris, at Saint Peter's Church,
> Shall happily make thee there a joyful bride.

_This is the really big worry — she's already married to Romeo, but she can't disobey her parents.

Following Steps — they're my favourite band...

The beauty of this step-by-step method is that you don't miss anything out. It may not be the most exciting thing in the world, but it gets you the marks — that's what matters. Don't just tell the story of the scene again — use it to help you write about the points from the task.

Finding Your Answer

Problems and reactions — that's what you're looking for. You need to go through the whole scene finding the bits that match the four points from the task — they're the key parts.

The Second Point's about Capulet and Juliet

Scoot through the scene until you get to the bit where Capulet comes in.

Don't forget — you're supposed to be looking at Juliet's problems and how she reacts to them.

Capulet doesn't speak to Juliet when he comes in — he speaks to his wife. When she tells him Juliet refuses the marriage, he explodes with anger.

> How, will she none? Doth she not give us thanks?
> Is she not proud?

Problem number 1 — Capulet wants her to marry Paris but she says no.

He can't believe she's refused — so he insults her and threatens to drag her there.

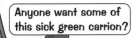

Anyone want some of this sick green carrion?

> Or I will drag thee on a hurdle thither.
> Out, you green sickness carrion! Out you baggage!

OUT YOU BAGGAGE!

Juliet answers back to her father. That's a big deal — she's only a child, and she's supposed to be completely obedient to her parents.

Here's how Juliet reacts to the problem of the marriage.

> JULIET   Good father, I beseech thee on my knees,
>   Hear me with patience but to speak a word.
>   [*She kneels down.*]

She even kneels down to beg him to listen — but he won't.

You need to think about what Juliet is doing here. Getting on her knees is a really desperate reaction to the problem.

Remember — it isn't just what the characters say, it's what they do as well.

Instead, he rages about the place — it even looks like he might hit Juliet when he says "my fingers itch". The Nurse tries to step in but Capulet insults her too. Eventually he makes a worse threat.

These measles are a nightmare.

I'm so itchy.

We work our fingers to the bone, scratching everyone else but does anyone ever think of us — oh no.

> I tell thee what; get thee to church o' Thursday
> Or never again look me in the face.

Suddenly Juliet's got a new problem — if she doesn't marry Paris, Capulet will throw her out of his house.

Capulet + Juliet = explosive reaction...

OK, this is where you really have to write about Juliet's reaction as well as what's happening. Write about what she does on stage as well as what she says. You can write about how Lord Capulet treats the Nurse, too — it's something else that puts more pressure on Juliet.

Finding the Answer

It's all about <u>finding</u> the right bits — you've got to <u>quote</u> them in your answer to <u>back up</u> what you're saying...

Next Point — the Nurse's Advice isn't Much Help

Look through the speech the Nurse makes <u>near the end</u> of the scene after Lady Capulet's gone. Juliet's <u>desperate</u> for some kind of help. The Nurse <u>means well</u>, but her advice <u>isn't</u> much use.

The Nurse compares Paris to Romeo — she's being totally practical. She tells Juliet to marry Paris even though Juliet is already married.

> Since the case so stands as it doth,
> I think it best you married with the County.
> O, he's a lovely gentleman!
> Romeo's a dishclout to him.

> Your first is dead—or 'twere as good he were
> As living here and you no use of him.

← *The Nurse says Romeo is <u>as good as dead</u> — she's making excuses for saying that Juliet ought to break her promises to Romeo and get married to Paris.*

Juliet's Reaction — She Pretends to be Comforted

Be careful here — Juliet says <u>one thing</u> when the Nurse is <u>still there</u>, and <u>something else</u> when the Nurse has <u>gone</u>.

This page needs a picture, but there's no room to swing a cat.

I'm not a cat.

> Well, thou hast comforted me marvellous much.
> Go in and tell my lady I am gone,
> Having displeased my father, to Lawrence' cell
> To make confession and be absolv'd.

Juliet pretends she's pleased with the Nurse's advice, and sorry for arguing with her father. She says she's going to confession — in fact she's going to ask Friar Lawrence for advice on what to do.

When the Nurse goes, Juliet shows her <u>true feelings</u>. She's speaking to the <u>audience</u> — there's no one else on stage.

> Ancient damnation! O most wicked fiend!

The Last Point is about the Whole Scene

Hole scene.

It's about <u>Juliet's situation</u> at the <u>end</u> of the scene — all the <u>problems</u> she has, and her <u>reaction</u> to them.

> If all else fail, myself have power to die.

Here's her <u>reaction</u> — it's pretty <u>extreme</u>.

Juliet's situation is <u>bad</u> — Romeo is in Mantua and can't help her, her parents want to force her to marry Paris, and even the Nurse is against her. There doesn't seem to be any solution — she says she'll go to see the Friar. If he can't help her, she'll <u>kill herself</u>.

Nurse's advice? — I prefer Doctor's orders...

This <u>doesn't</u> have to be hard work. The main thing is to <u>read</u> the scene <u>carefully</u> and make <u>clear notes</u>. I've written my notes out in full so you can read them — you can make them <u>shorter</u> to save time. Don't forget — you've got to find quotations to <u>back up</u> the points in your answer.

Planning Your Answer

You've got to write about <u>everything</u> they ask you about, or you'll end up losing out. <u>Planning</u> your answer is the <u>only way</u> you'll be sure of giving yourself <u>enough to write</u>.

You Get 10-15 Minutes to Read and Plan

After you've <u>read</u> the scene to find the important bits, it's time to <u>make a plan</u>.

MAKE NOTES: Jot down things that look <u>relevant</u> to the task.

No choice — her father will <u>disown</u> her if she doesn't marry Paris.

Plan-et man

NOTE DOWN QUOTATIONS: You have to <u>give quotations</u> if you want good marks — so make sure you <u>note down</u> <u>where</u> to find any useful ones in the scene.

The Nurse has gone, and Juliet shows her <u>true feelings</u> to the <u>audience</u> (line 235). ◀

<u>Don't</u> put the <u>whole</u> quotation in your notes — that'll waste time. Just put down the <u>line number</u>.

<u>15 minutes</u> is plenty of time to <u>read the scene</u> and <u>write a plan</u>. It's <u>not</u> enough time to mess about — so get that plan <u>sorted</u>.

The Two Key Points about Planning

If you <u>don't</u> plan your answer properly, there'll be a couple of <u>nasty surprises</u> lurking around the corner.

① <u>Don't</u> start writing until you've got <u>enough</u> to say — you don't want to <u>run out</u> of things to write after 20 minutes.

Aaaaargh - follow the path of proper planning you should!

PLANNING

Whatever you do, <u>don't</u> start writing without a good idea of <u>what</u> you're going to say. That means you need to <u>plan</u> it first.

② Make sure you <u>don't</u> run out of time without answering <u>all</u> the points of the task.

You've <u>only</u> got an hour so use it carefully — you've got <u>four points</u> to write about, so give each one <u>15 minutes</u>. Time yourself so you don't spend <u>too long</u> on one point.

Sowing essay seeds — no that's planting an essay...

Planning's important for <u>any</u> kind of question. With these 'writing about a character' questions it's easy to spend <u>too much</u> time writing about <u>one</u> of the points just because there's a <u>fair old</u> <u>amount</u> to write <u>about</u>. Work out <u>how much</u> time each point should take, and <u>stick</u> to it.

Starting Your Answer

Phew — if you've done your <u>reading</u> and <u>planning</u> properly, you'll know what to write about. This page is about making a <u>good start</u> so the rest of your answer will flow nice and <u>smoothly</u>.

Don't be Boring — Give a Short Introduction

The main thing with this kind of answer is not to let it get <u>boring</u>.

Give a little <u>introduction</u> with your basic answer to the question <u>before</u> you launch into writing about the four main points.

Use the Exact Words of the Task

A great way of making it look like you're getting <u>right in there</u> and answering the question is to start your answer with the <u>same words</u> that the <u>task</u> uses.

The task (page 59) says "What <u>problems</u> does Juliet <u>face</u> in this scene" — and the first sentence uses the same words.

Get right to the <u>nitty-gritty</u>. You've got to write about her <u>problems</u> and her <u>reactions</u> — so you need to get <u>both</u> into the start of your answer.

> *Juliet faces several serious <u>problems</u> in this scene. Her life goes from bad to worse, as Romeo leaves for Mantua, and her parents tell her she has to marry Paris. Even the Nurse tells her to forget about Romeo.*
>
> *Juliet <u>reacts</u> by hiding her true feelings from everyone. Only at the end of the scene does she say what she's really thinking — either the Friar will help her or she will kill herself.*

Don't bang on and on — keep the introduction <u>snappy</u>.
Don't write much more than this. A couple of <u>short paragraphs</u> is enough.

Examiners Like a Good Beginning

I'm afraid so — all that rubbish you hear about how <u>first impressions count</u> is <u>true</u>. Start your answer <u>confidently</u> — it counts for a lot with the Examiners.

I said "good beginning" not "hyena in a dressing gown"

I <u>know</u> I can win!

Now that's what I call a confident starter...

A good beginning — once upon a time...

Don't spend <u>too much</u> time here. Go straight in there with <u>clear points</u> saying what the <u>main problems</u> are, and how Juliet <u>reacts</u> to them. It shows you've understood the <u>task</u> and the <u>scene</u>.

Writing the Answer

This is the nasty bit — turning your plan into a <u>clear</u> answer. <u>Don't</u> just retell the story of the scene — you <u>won't</u> get any marks for that. Stick to <u>answering</u> the points of the <u>task</u>.

Stick <u>to the</u> Point <u>about Juliet's</u> Problems

Use a <u>new paragraph</u> for each <u>new point</u> you make.

But my problem is I'm stuck to a point.

You need to give lots of <u>quotations</u> too.

When Lady Capulet arrives, Juliet finds herself in a difficult situation. She is crying, but she can't let her mother know the real reason. Her marriage to Romeo is a secret, and must be kept secret all the more because Romeo was the "villain" who killed Tybalt.

Lady Capulet immediately assumes that Juliet is crying over Tybalt's death. "Evermore weeping for your cousin's death?" Juliet reacts by being deliberately vague in her answers: "Yet let me weep for such a feeling loss." She's still talking about Romeo, but her mother still thinks she's crying for Tybalt.

Don't Forget <u>to Write about</u> How She Reacts

Juliet only shows her real reaction to the audience, not to her mother. When Lady Capulet calls Romeo a villain, Juliet says to herself, "Villain and he be many miles asunder" (line 81). That shows she's still on Romeo's side, even though she's pretending to hate him for murdering her cousin.

Make sure you explain <u>how</u> the quotations <u>link</u> to Juliet's <u>problems</u> or her <u>reaction</u>.

Sunder | Oh so that's a Sunder

You've got to say what Juliet <u>means</u>.

What a clever pint.

This is quite a <u>clever point</u>. You need your <u>wits</u> about you to spot this sort of thing.

When Lady Capulet tells Juliet about the arranged wedding, Juliet reacts by refusing to do it. "I will not marry yet." She simply says she will not obey her parents' wishes, saying it has all happened too fast: "I wonder at this haste" (line 118).

The real reason she won't get married is because she's already married to Romeo — she can't marry someone else. But she doesn't tell her mother this directly. Instead she says it in a roundabout way:

> I will not marry yet, and when I do, I swear
> It shall be Romeo, whom you know I hate,
> Rather than Paris.   (lines 121-3)

Lady Capulet doesn't realise that Juliet is telling her she's in love with Romeo, but the audience knows what she means.

See how Juliet reacts — add plutonium...

Juliet's <u>problems</u> and <u>how she reacts</u> — that's what you're writing about. <u>Don't</u> get <u>sidetracked</u>.

Writing the Answer

So much to say, and so little time — it's really easy to get <u>bogged down</u> in your answer. Make sure you don't start <u>confusing</u> different points. You've got to keep them <u>clear</u>.

Keep Your Points Clear and Easy to Follow

<u>Link</u> your paragraphs together with phrases like '<u>in contrast</u>' and '<u>on the other hand</u>'.

The word "reacts" is in there — it <u>shows</u> you're still <u>sticking</u> to the task.

> *In contrast, Juliet's argument with her father is much more tense and confrontational. Children in Shakespeare's time were supposed to be completely obedient to their parents, so the fact that Juliet reacts by answering back and arguing is very significant. Capulet's first line: "How how, how how, chop logic, what is this?" (line 149) shows that he is shocked at his daughter's behaviour.*

<u>Every point</u> you make should have a <u>quotation</u> to back it up.

Don't Try to Write About Everything At Once

You've got to <u>make sure</u> that you write your points in a way that the <u>examiners</u> can <u>follow</u>.

Don't <u>confuse</u> two <u>different points</u> in the same paragraph — keep them in <u>separate ones</u>.

This point's about Capulet's <u>confrontation</u> with Juliet.

> *Capulet rants and rages and finally storms out, threatening to throw Juliet onto the streets and swearing to disown her: "For by my soul, I ne'er acknowledge thee." (line 193)*
> *When he has gone, and Lady Capulet leaves, Juliet turns to the only person there who knows about her marriage. She begs the Nurse for advice: "O Nurse, how shall this be prevented?" (line 204)*

But this is about the <u>Nurse's advice</u> — they need to stay <u>separate</u>.

Don't try and write about everything at once.

Don't Contradict Yourself

Don't get caught out saying <u>one thing</u> in one part of your essay, and the <u>opposite</u> in another part.

He's right. Wrong.

> *Capulet is being cruel and unfair to Juliet.*

> *Capulet is right to be angry with Juliet.*

If the first one is <u>true</u>, then the other one <u>can't</u> be. The examiners <u>won't know</u> what to think — and you'll definitely <u>lose marks</u> for that. Be careful <u>not</u> to contradict your own points.

Don't get caught out — it looks like rain...

Keep your answer <u>clear</u> and <u>contradiction-free</u>. You've got a <u>whole hour</u> to <u>fit</u> everything in.

Section Six — Writing About Characters

Ending Your Answer

This is the bit most people <u>don't</u> get round to doing — <u>ending</u> their answers <u>properly</u>.

You Need to Sum Up Your Points at the End

You've got to leave time for a <u>proper ending</u> to your essay — it's your <u>last chance</u> to show the examiners <u>how well</u> you've done the task. You need to <u>show</u> them that you've done <u>all</u> the parts.

This Question's Great — It Helps You to Sum Up

The last point from the task is about <u>Juliet's situation</u> at the end of the scene. This is a real <u>gift</u> — it gives you a chance to <u>go through</u> the main <u>problems</u> at the end of the scene and her <u>reaction</u> (what she says she's going to do about them).

Here's a <u>summary</u> of the main problems.

Vein problems

> *Juliet's situation at the end of the scene is desperate. The problems she had at the beginning of the scene have all become much worse. Romeo is still banished from Verona and she might never see him again, but now she's being forced to marry someone else as well. This would be both a crime and a sin — she would be "forsworn", because she swore in her marriage vow to Romeo not to marry anyone else. Unfortunately, if she doesn't do as her father tells her, she'll be thrown out onto the streets.*

And here's how Juliet <u>reacts</u> to them.

> *Her reaction to the situation is simple — everyone has deserted her, even the Nurse. The only person who can help is Friar Lawrence, so she decides to go to him. At the same time, she doesn't seem to be holding out much hope — she's ready to kill herself if the Friar can't help her: "If all else fail, myself have power to die." (line 242) There doesn't seem to be another way out.*

See if you can <u>finish</u> with a final sentence that <u>rounds</u> everything off.

Don't Panic if You Run Out of Time

Whatever you do, don't stop in the <u>middle</u> of a sentence and leave it hanging there. You'll still have time to write <u>one last sentence</u> (two if you're lucky) that <u>sums up</u> your main answer.

Two quick <u>final sentences</u> — that's all you need.

> *Juliet thinks the Nurse has turned against her.*
> *Juliet's main problem in this scene is that her parents want her to marry Paris, but she's secretly already married to Romeo. Capulet threatens to disown her, and she reacts by going to see the Friar and thinking about killing herself.*

This play's a bit cheesy — but the question's grate...

<u>Ending</u> your answer properly is a way to <u>pick up marks</u> — the examiners'll see you <u>know your stuff</u>.

Revision Summary

Writing about characters is easier than it looks. The secret is to make sure you cover all the parts of the question and stick to the point. As long as you read the scene carefully and remember to quote from it, you should pick up plenty of marks. In fact, you may as well get into the habit now, by having a go at these revision questions. You know the score — have a go at the questions, then look up any that you can't answer. By the time you've finished, you should be able to answer the whole lot without looking back once.

1) What are the three things you need to look out for to answer the question?

2) What's the best way to answer this kind of question?

3) What are the three steps you should follow?

4) Why shouldn't you just tell the story of the scene again?

5) Apart from what the characters say, what do you have to think about?

6) Why do you have to give quotations?

7) Give two reasons for planning your answer.

8) How can you start the introduction to your answer?

9) Why do examiners like a good beginning?

10) When should you use a new paragraph?

11) What should every point you make have with it?

12) Why should you avoid contradicting yourself?

13) Why do you need to sum up your main points?

14) What should you do if you run out of time for your answer?

With five minutes of the exam to go, William realised his mistake.

Writing As A Character

These tasks <u>look</u> straightforward, but it's really <u>hard</u> to get marks for them.
This section will help you get <u>more marks</u> — but it <u>won't</u> make it easy.

Character Questions Are A Real Nightmare

The <u>nasty</u> thing about writing as a character is that you have to do <u>two jobs</u> at once.

1) The <u>first</u> job is straightforward — you write about the scene just like you do for any other type of task.

2) The second job is more <u>tricky</u>. You have to pretend <u>you</u> are a character from the scene as you write your answer.

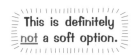

This is definitely <u>not</u> a soft option.

Bob's Pizza 'n' Carpentry

Bob liked to do two jobs at once.

3) You <u>can't</u> use your <u>ordinary</u> essay style. You have to write like <u>you're the character</u>.

4) You have to think hard about what the <u>character's</u> ideas on the scene would be. Their ideas could be <u>different</u> from yours.

Here's How You Go About Doing Them

> Imagine you are Friar Lawrence. Write down your thoughts and feelings after your conversation with Romeo.

Don't worry about the <u>details</u> of this question just yet.
You need to know some <u>general</u> stuff <u>first</u>.

There are always <u>two</u> things you have to do in <u>this kind</u> of task:

General Stuff's SAT plan

"Shakespeare with Military Precision"

 1 Write about a scene from the play.

Make <u>sensible comments</u> which are <u>closely</u> based on the scene and backed up with good quotes.

2 Pretend to be one of the characters — make it sound like you were <u>really</u> there.

Don't <u>just</u> describe what you did and said in the scene. Describe what you <u>think</u> and <u>feel</u> about the things <u>the other characters</u> said and did.

Say something about the <u>action</u> as well as the <u>words</u>.

Character questions — what are they like?...

It's well worth knowing <u>which</u> questions are particularly tricky <u>before</u> you go into the exam. Learn the basics of what this kind of question wants you to do — then you'll be <u>better prepared</u>.

Get To Grips With The Task

OK, so you've heard this before — but make sure you remember it when you're actually <u>doing</u> the test. Don't write a thing till you've <u>read</u> the <u>question paper</u> and the <u>extract from the play</u>.

Have A *Good Look* At The Task

<u>First</u> they tell you <u>what scene</u> you have to write about.
You'll get a copy of the scene to <u>read</u> and <u>quote</u> from.

Act 3 Scene 3

Romeo has been banished from Verona. He thinks he will never see Juliet again.
In this scene Friar Lawrence persuades Romeo that his situation is not hopeless.

It'll <u>really help</u> if you already have a rough idea of what the scene's about. Use Section Five to learn what happens in each scene.

These sentences tell you the <u>basics</u> about what happens in the scene.

This bit in <u>bold</u> is the <u>actual task</u> you have to do.

Imagine you are Friar Lawrence. Write down your thoughts and feelings after your conversation with Romeo.

The task is to write about <u>Act 3 Scene 3</u>, as though you are <u>Friar Lawrence</u>.
You have to imagine <u>his</u> thoughts and feelings about what happens in the scene.

You could begin:

Today the Prince banished Romeo for killing Tybalt.
Romeo was in a terrible state.
I hope I managed to talk some sense into him...

Start off with what's just <u>happened</u>.

Luckily *They Give You Some* Hints

These points are dead useful — you can use them as your <u>essay plan</u>. There'll be <u>more</u> about that on P.73.

Before you begin to write you should think about:

* Romeo's emotional state at the beginning of the scene and how it changes;
* what the Friar says to change the way Romeo feels;
* the problems Romeo and Juliet still face.

Jobs in Berkshire — Reading tasks...

<u>Don't</u> skip this stage out. It might not seem important, but it is. Not reading the question properly and then writing the <u>wrong thing</u> must be the <u>stupidest</u> way to miss out on the marks.

Read The Scene

The worst thing you can do is make good points about the wrong things.
Looking at the question carefully will help you pick out the right information from the scene.

Just Whizz Through The Scene At First

While you read the scene make notes — as messy as you like.
It means you won't waste your ideas by forgetting them.

Skim through the scene. Check who's in it, and look at the stage directions to get a rough idea of what's going on.

> Romeo at Friar Lawrence's cell
> Friar comes back and says he's banished
> Romeo SO upset
> Nurse comes to ask Romeo to go to Juliet
> Romeo persuaded to go and leaves

Then Have A Look In More Detail

Friar: Romeo, come forth, come forth, thou fearful man:
Affliction is enamor'd of thy parts,
And thou art wedded to calamity.

1) Read the scene in full. If there's a bit you can't understand, mark it and come back to it later.

You might decide it's not that important, or you might find you understand it second time round.

2) Mark the margin next to anything you think you'll want to write about later.

Friar: This is dear mercy and thou seest it not.
Romeo: 'Tis torture, and not mercy.

Use Those Handy Hints From The Examiners

Go through the examiners' suggestions for things to 'think about' one at a time.
Look in the scene for things to say about each hint.

As you make your notes, include relevant bits of the scene.
You can quote them in the answer to make your point more convincing.

That's 'handy hint', not 'handy mint'...

Decide how you think the Friar feels about the things you are describing, and note that too.

Moor detail — windswept hills, gorse, sheep...

Read the scene carefully — it's the only place you'll get to look for the answer. You don't want to miss anything important out, so go through the scene with the question in your mind, and look for all the relevant bits. Remember, though, some bits are more relevant than others.

Make Some Notes

Your <u>notes</u> are an <u>important</u> part of doing the task.
Don't start writing till you've got enough in your notes to give a <u>full</u> answer.

Look at The Whole Scene

Start by making notes on the <u>first</u> hint.
That's the first thing they want you to write about:

Felix preferred not to look at the whole scene

- Romeo's emotional state at the beginning of the scene and how it changes;

They ask you to look at how Romeo's emotional state <u>changes</u>.

That means looking at the <u>whole scene</u> to see what the changes are.

Think About How The Friar Feels

You're writing as the <u>Friar</u>, remember, so work out how <u>he</u> feels each time Romeo's emotions change.

How do I <u>feel</u>?
That's a good question...

BEGINNING: R upset about being banished.
Says it's worse than death
        "Be merciful, say 'death';
For exile hath more terror in his look."
F tries make R feel better. Won't listen.
"Thou canst not speak of that thou dost not feel."

F <u>surprised</u> at reaction — thinks death worse.
Then thinks R doesn't realise how lucky he is. Quite <u>angry</u>.
"O deadly sin! O rude unthankfulness!"

You need <u>quotes</u> to back up each point.

NURSE ARRIVES: R lying on ground in tears
"with his own tears made drunk".

drunk — F thinks R has lost control of himself.

<u>Split</u> the scene up into <u>bits</u> to show the <u>changes</u> in Romeo's emotions clearly.

END: After F's long speech R much happier.
He feels he has behaved wrongly — "bid my sweet prepare to chide".
He's also v. excited about seeing Juliet — "a joy past joy calls out to me".

F <u>knows</u> his speech changed R's mind — pleased/relieved.
Says R will go to Juliet. R hasn't said so yet. Asks to shake hands with R before he goes — being friendly. Not cross any more.

When you write the answer, remember to include your points about how the Friar <u>felt</u> as well as <u>what happened</u>.

Your notes <u>don't</u> need to be <u>neat</u> or <u>detailed</u> or even in proper sentences — they're just a quick <u>reminder</u> of what to write in your answer.

Tie ropes together — make some knots...

This is the part of the process where you work out what your <u>answer</u> is. Take each point one at a time and go through the scene — look for bits that show you how the Friar <u>feels</u> about it.

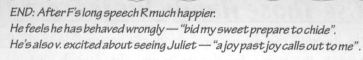

Section Seven — Writing As A Character

Make More Notes

Don't start writing an answer till you've looked at every part of the question.
There's no point in starting to write before you know you've got something to say.

For This One Read The *Friar's Speeches*

• what the Friar says to change the way Romeo feels;

You need to go through the whole scene again,
looking closely at Friar Lawrence's speeches.

> FRIAR'S LONG SPEECH: R tries kill himself —
> his lowest point in scene. Nurse snatches away dagger.
> F wants to persuade R death a bad choice.
> Tries make R ashamed —
> "Unseemly woman in a seeming man"
> and tells him off —
> "Thou hast amaz'd me! By my holy order,
> I thought thy disposition better temper'd."
>
> FRIAR FEELS: surprised at R's extreme reaction.
> F knows R well but didn't expect him to try suicide.
> Angry with his unmanly behaviour.
>
> LATER: relieved that Romeo didn't kill himself

> R doesn't want to die any more.
> Now F wants to persuade R be happy.
> Gives many reasons,
> e.g. not dead, J not dead, enemy Tybalt is dead.
>
> FRIAR FEELS: Glad R not as upset, now wants to make R see
> he has good reasons to be happy.
>
> LATER: Hopes R's happiness will last.

Think about how the Friar would feel at the time,
and how he'd feel looking back on the scene.

The Last Bit's About *What Happens Next*

This is about: • the problems Romeo and Juliet still face.

In this last point, think about how the play ends. It'll help you
think of things that could go wrong for Romeo and Juliet.

> R can't be caught in Verona — will be executed.
> F worried he will be caught tonight, or tomorrow if he stays with J.
> "Either be gone before the watch be set,
> Or by the break of day disguis'd from hence."

Well done, Team A,
that's exactly what
happened next.

You still need to back your ideas
up with quotes from this scene.

> F told R that he could come back from Mantua one day:
> "With twenty hundred thousand times more joy
> Than thou went'st forth in lamentation."
> Hopes things really will turn out so well — unlikely as
> long as the feud continues.

What happens next — a question of thought...

Make sure you know what you're looking for. Keep the words of the question in your mind.
Whatever you do, don't forget to note down how you think the Friar feels for each part of the
question. Jot down some quotes, too — you're gonna have to put them in your answer.

Putting Your Answer In Order

Your answer needs a <u>beginning</u>, a <u>middle</u> with a new paragraph for every new idea, and an <u>ending</u>.

Get Your Ideas In Order

1) The <u>easiest</u> way to put your ideas <u>in order</u> is to <u>follow</u> the order of the <u>hints</u>.

2) Write an <u>opening paragraph</u>, then put your ideas down in the order of the hints.

3) Leave enough time at the end of the test to write a <u>good ending</u> — one that <u>sums up</u> the main points from your answer.

That gives you a <u>plan</u> for your answer that looks like this:

Planning's <u>not</u> a waste of time. You only do one task in this test, so you need to be sure you've got it <u>just right</u>.

* Opening paragraph

* Romeo's emotional state

* Friar's advice to Romeo

* problems for Romeo and Juliet

* Ending — summary of main points

They Give You The First Few Lines

In the instructions for the task they <u>suggest</u> how you could start your <u>opening paragraph</u>.

*Today the Prince banished Romeo for killing Tybalt. Romeo was in a terrible state.
I hope I managed to talk some sense into him...*

It's a really <u>good idea</u> to start your piece with the suggested words.

<u>Copy</u> them out, and then make your first point.

Link the suggested words in with your own first words, so it sounds like one piece of writing.

Today the Prince banished Romeo for killing Tybalt. Romeo was in a terrible state. I hope I managed to talk some sense into him. I tried my hardest to make Romeo realise he's lucky to be alive. He wouldn't listen to me at all to start with, though.

You don't <u>have</u> to use the suggested words though.
If you think of a way to start that's <u>easier for you</u> then use that.

A good start these days is hard to find...

A <u>good start</u> is really important. In this kind of task they give you a start, which makes it easier.
Make sure that what you write next carries on in the <u>same kind of style</u> or it'll all fall a bit flat.

Answering The Question

Now you've got started it's time to <u>dive</u> into making your points.
Don't forget — you're writing as though <u>you</u> are Friar Lawrence.

The *First* Paragraph — *Romeo's Feelings*

The first paragraph should be on how Romeo feels at the <u>beginning</u> of the scene.
You might need <u>two</u> or <u>three</u> more paragraphs to describe <u>each change</u> in Romeo's feelings.

Try to make your first paragraph <u>follow on</u> from the introduction.

...I tried my hardest to make Romeo realise he's lucky to be alive. He wouldn't listen to me at all to start with though.
He claimed that "exile hath more terror in his look than death". It made no difference what I said — all Romeo could think about was being parted from Juliet. He couldn't see any reason to be happy.

Make sure you always say "<u>I</u>" — <u>not</u> "Friar Lawrence".

...The Nurse told Romeo Juliet was in tears all the time, calling out Tybalt's and Romeo's names. Romeo realised how unhappy he had made Juliet. He was afraid even the sound of his name was painful to her, that it:
"Did murther her as that name's cursed hand
Murder'd her kinsman."
This thought was too much for him, and he tried to stab himself...

This paragraph is about how Romeo's feelings change <u>when the Nurse arrives</u>.

Stick in plenty of <u>relevant</u> quotes — the examiners love them.

On with the Next Part *— Use Those* Notes

Go through your <u>notes</u>, and find the part about what the Friar says to Romeo.

This time, concentrate on how the Friar <u>talks Romeo round</u>, not on how Romeo feels.

Romeo's ungratefulness to God and the Prince for sparing his life made me quite angry. I told him his attitude was "deadly sin" and "rude unthankfulness". But Romeo had an answer for everything. When I said being banished was "mercy", Romeo replied, "'Tis torture and not mercy." I was determined to talk Romeo out of his misery, so I kept going...

Put <u>all</u> the quotes in quotation marks.

This answer's OK — well, it's friarly good...

This is where you'll start to see the benefit of making <u>plenty of notes</u>. You'll have done all the <u>hard thinking</u>, so now you can concentrate on writing your answer really well. Remember, <u>half</u> your final mark is on how good your <u>writing</u> is. Don't throw away marks on <u>daft mistakes</u>.

Answering The Question

Another Important bit — When Romeo Cheers Up

The Friar hasn't explained how he changed Romeo's mind yet.
You need to find the <u>moment</u> when you think Romeo's feelings <u>lift</u>.

Make your answer <u>more fun</u> to read by including little
bits of <u>action</u> as well as talking about what people say.

Make it
FUN
to read

> Romeo went very quiet after the Nurse snatched the dagger
> away from him. I realised it was no use telling him banishment was a
> good thing, so I pointed out all the other reasons he's got to be
> happy — he's alive, his enemy's dead... the sort of things that would
> be obvious to him if he wasn't so worked up...

> ...I think it was when I pointed out that he should be spending
> tonight with Juliet that he finally cheered up. I stopped trying
> to persuade him to be happy, and just ordered him to go to
> Juliet: "Go get thee to thy love as was decreed"...

This paragraph uses a <u>quote</u> to
show exactly what the Friar said
to change the way Romeo feels.

The Last Bit — Look into your Crystal Ball

The <u>final</u> part of the task is about the <u>future</u>.
You have to imagine what the Friar thinks could happen <u>next</u>.

> I told Romeo I hoped he could come back from Mantua soon:
>   "With twenty hundred thousand times more joy
>   Than thou went'st forth in lamentation."
> Perhaps I shouldn't have said it — it's not likely as long as the
> feud continues. The Capulets won't be quick to forgive Romeo for
> killing Tybalt.
>   Romeo and Juliet might spend tonight together, but it could
> be months before they see each other again. I only hope the
> Watch don't catch Romeo before he gets to the Capulets'
> house...

Remember, the
Friar <u>doesn't</u>
know the whole
story — he only
knows it up to
<u>Act 3 Scene 3</u>.

You <u>can</u> say Friar Lawrence is worried Romeo
will be killed if the <u>Capulets</u> get their hands on
him, because it's <u>nearly</u> happened before.

You <u>can't</u> say he's worried Juliet will be <u>kidnapped</u> by <u>Sicilian</u>
<u>merchants</u> because <u>nothing</u> remotely like that happens in the play.

SATs — they're what the future holds for you...

When you've got Friar Lawrence thinking about the future <u>don't</u> make up anything <u>daft</u>. Make
sure it's something likely. You can use <u>your</u> knowledge of the rest of the play, but remember
the Friar isn't <u>clairvoyant</u> — he won't know every single thing that's going to happen.

Finishing It All Off

You can make your work even better by making sure you finish it off well.

Give Your Answer A Definite Ending

A definite ending gives you a chance to sum up all your points.
It will impress the examiner, too. It makes your piece look complete.

Aha!
There's my end!

I only hope the Watch don't catch Romeo before he gets to the Capulets' house.

Romeo's happy now, but I'm afraid his happiness won't last. Next time he tries killing himself I might not be there to talk him out of it. His feelings are so extreme — happy one minute and ready to die the next — that you can never be sure he won't rush into another terrible situation.

This is the end of the paragraph on problems for Romeo and Juliet.

The ending sums up by talking about Romeo's mood swings in the scene, and hoping they won't lead to trouble in future.

Check For Silly Blunders

Plan to have a couple of minutes left over at the end, and use them to check for mistakes.

Check the spelling of all character names.

Check you haven't spelt words in quotes wrong.

There are no excuses for this. All you have to do is copy them carefully from the test paper.

There's no excuse for that either.

Don't drift off into normal essay style.

Don't forget grammar, spelling and punctuation.

If you don't write as though you are the Friar you're not doing the task.

You get marked on them too. Make sure they're as good as they can be.

Correct any mistakes neatly — you don't want to make your writing difficult to read.

Oh, No, I've Run Out Of Time

You might not have enough time to write a whole paragraph as your ending.
If not, try to sum up what you've written in one sentence.

For this task you could just write:

I've done my best to make Romeo happy, but I'm afraid his feelings are so extreme that his happiness won't last.

That's not a brilliant ending, but it's better than nothing at all.

The end is near — The final curtain...

If you run out of time in the Exam, don't just stop. You'll have enough time to write one last sentence that sums up what you were going to say — and that's better than nothing. If you have time to check for silly mistakes, brilliant — but try not to make any of them in the first place.

Revision Summary

OK, it's time for another portion of revision summary questions. This lot will test how well you've learned to plan and write answers to those tricky "Imagine you're..." questions. You know the drill by now — go through 'em all, look back if there are any you don't know, but don't give up until you can answer every single last one. Off you go — learn and enjoy...

1) Why are questions that ask you to imagine you're a character so difficult?

2) What two things do you have to do in every "Imagine you are..." task?

3) When you read through the scene, should you pay attention to the stage directions?

4) Should you: a) *Go through the whole scene and make notes on absolutely every little thing?*
    or   b) *Make notes on each hint one by one?*

5) What else must you write about, apart from what happens in the scene?

6) Should you write about: a) *What the character said at the time?*
                                  b) *What they thought about it afterwards?*
                                  c) *What they felt about it at the time AND looking back on it?*

7) When you're writing as a character, do you still need to quote from the scene?

8) Is planning: a) *a complete waste of time?*   b) *the way to get your answer looking good?*

9) Is it a good idea to use the suggested first few lines?

10) If you use the suggested first lines, how should your answer carry on?

11) When you write, should you use "I" or "he"/"she" to talk about your character?

12) What makes your answer more fun to read and gets you more marks?

                                  a) *Talking about the action on stage*
                                  b) *Jolly pictures in the margin*
                                  c) *Dancing hamsters*

13) When you write about what a character thinks will happen next, do you have to be completely true to what really happens later in the play?

14) What must you make sure you don't do?

15) Why do you need a good ending?

16) Why should you plan to have a couple of minutes left over at the end?

17) What four silly mistakes should you especially check for?

18) What should you do if you run out of time?

Running out of time...
That's <u>almost</u> funny...

Understanding Mood Tasks

Mood tasks ask how a scene makes you feel. They usually ask you to explain how Shakespeare gives a scene a particular atmosphere.

Mood Tasks are Easier Than They Look

The thing about these tasks is they're not just about the characters or the story — they're about how the audience feels when they watch the scene, and why they feel like that.

Here's a typical mood task...

The key words are "tense" and "exciting".

> Describe how Shakespeare makes the scene tense and exciting.

It sounds more tricky because they say "Shakespeare makes...". All it means is "This scene is tense and exciting. Why?".

Don't forget the handy hints — these are the things to write about in your answer.

In your answer pay particular attention to:

— the opening of the scene (lines 1-48);

— the interaction between Mercutio and Tybalt;

— Romeo's words and actions;

— the arrival of the Prince at the end.

I am NOT in a mood!

Looks to me like something's got your goat.

These hints tell you which parts of the scene to pay attention to.

The Scene's Got Tense and Exciting Bits

Some parts of the scene are tense. Some parts are exciting. And some parts are tense and exciting.

Tense   Exciting

1) Think about what "tense" and "exciting" mean, and especially about what the difference is between them.

2) Imagine the play being acted on a stage, and which bits would make the audience feel tense or excited. Think about how you feel when you read it.

3) You'll have to decide why they make the audience tense or excited.

"Tense" means strained or nervous — like when you're expecting something bad to happen.

The scene only gets "exciting" when things really do start happening.

Teepee and circus marquee — that's too tense...

Make sure you read the question carefully and pick out exactly what it's asking you to do. The hints underneath the question are very important — they can be incredibly helpful.

Looking At The Scene

There are three main ways Shakespeare could make the scene tense and exciting.
Make sure you look out for all of these when you read the scene.

First Things First — What Happens

Remember — the stage directions tell you what people do onstage.
They help you to imagine what you would see when it's acted out.

Skim read the scene, looking at the stage directions to find tense or exciting events.

1) Here's a scuffle.

This way to the stage please.

[*Romeo steps between them.*]
Hold, Tybalt! Good Mercutio!
[*Tybalt under Romeo's arm thrusts Mercutio in.*
Away Tybalt with his followers.]

2) Here's a stabbing.

3) And here a whole load of people run off the stage.

Check What Characters Say

Now read the scene again. Look at what the characters say to each other, and decide if it makes the scene more tense or exciting.

Benvolio's just finished pleading with the Prince to spare Romeo's life — but Lady Capulet wants Romeo's blood as revenge for Tybalt's death.

LADY CAPULET   I beg for justice, which thou, Prince, must give;
Romeo slew Tybalt, Romeo must not live.

I'm not saying anything!

It's tense because we don't know if the Prince is going to decide to execute Romeo or not — his life's in the balance.

Look at the Way People Say Things

You need to think about the way people talk — that can make the scene tense and exciting too.

Here Romeo talks in really polite and friendly language, even though Tybalt's been insulting him:

...And so, good Capulet, which name I tender
As dearly as mine own, be satisfied.

1) Romeo's being polite because he wants to avoid a fight with Tybalt. Mercutio and Tybalt think he's being a wimp.

2) That makes this bit tense because you're waiting to see how Tybalt and Mercutio will react.

Skim reading — 99% fat free...

Read the scene once for each of the three things in turn — what happens, what the characters say to each other, and the language that Shakespeare uses. Stage directions help with the first one.

Section Eight — Writing About The Mood

Reading In Detail

Finding the <u>right bits</u> — that's what reading in detail is all about. Remember — you <u>don't</u> have to understand every single word, but you <u>do</u> have to give <u>quotations</u> in your answer.

Find the Bits You Think are Tense or Exciting

You need to be thinking about how the scene <u>looks onstage</u> — where the characters are <u>standing</u>, what <u>moods</u> they're in and the <u>way</u> they're speaking.

The scene <u>starts</u> with Benvolio telling Mercutio that if they don't go home they are <u>sure</u> to get into a fight.

> I'm mad for it, me.

Stirring the Mad Blood

| BENVOLIO | I pray thee, good Mercutio, let's retire. The day is hot, the Capels are abroad, And if we meet we shall not scape a brawl, For now, these hot days, is the mad blood stirring. |

Straightaway the scene <u>feels tense</u> — it's a <u>hot</u> day, and we <u>know</u> that the Capulets are <u>around somewhere</u>. It's almost like Benvolio <u>knows</u> what's going to happen.

While Benvolio sounds <u>worried</u>, Mercutio acts as if he <u>doesn't care</u>. He starts making long speeches <u>teasing</u> Benvolio.

It seems like Mercutio actually <u>wants</u> to get into a fight — he <u>doesn't care</u> what the <u>reason</u> is.

| MERCUTIO | Nay, and there were two such, we should have none shortly, for one would kill the other. Thou? why, thou wilt quarrel with a man that hath a hair less or a hair more in his beard than thou hast... |

Things Change When Tybalt Turns Up

Up till now, Mercutio's been all mouth and no trousers — he's only <u>talked</u> about quarrelling. When Tybalt turns up after line 34, suddenly the mood <u>changes</u>. It all gets much <u>more tense</u>. Tybalt tries to be <u>polite</u>, but Mercutio starts being <u>rude</u> to him.

Mercutio's <u>egging Tybalt on</u> to a fight.

> Come and have a go if you think you're hard enough...

MERCUTIO	And but one word with one of us? Couple it with something, make it a word and a blow.
TYBALT	You shall find me apt enough to that, sir, and you will give me occasion.
MERCUTIO	Could you not take some occasion without giving?
TYBALT	Mercutio, thou consortest with Romeo—
MERCUTIO	Consort! what, dost thou make us minstrels?

Here he <u>interrupts</u> Tybalt — he's trying to wind him up.

<u>Onstage</u> the characters could be standing <u>face to face</u>, or circling round each other. That would <u>add</u> to the tension.

82

Reading In Detail

It's easy enough to say, "Go through it in detail", but sometimes the <u>language</u> can get really <u>strange</u> — and before you know it, you've got yourself well and truly <u>confused</u>.

You <u>Don't</u> Have to Understand <u>Every</u> Word...

Hurrah — the examiners <u>don't</u> expect you to understand every single word. They're interested in <u>how well</u> you do the task. The <u>bits you choose</u> to write about are <u>up to you</u> — as long as they're <u>relevant</u> to the task. You <u>don't</u> have time to write about everything.

You've Got to <u>Follow</u> the <u>Gist</u> of the Scene

Here's a <u>difficult bit</u> of the scene — some of the words are really <u>weird</u>. But it's also a really <u>important bit</u>. You need to be able to <u>pick out</u> the <u>important parts</u>.

This is <u>important</u> — Romeo's just <u>refused</u> to fight Tybalt. Mercutio thinks he's being a <u>coward</u> by surrendering.

This bit <u>isn't</u> important — it <u>doesn't matter</u> if you <u>don't know</u> what 'alla stoccata' means. It's nothing but a <u>fancy fencing term</u>.

Alla Stoccata!

MERCUTIO   O calm, dishonourable, vile submission!
              'Alla stoccata' carries it away. [*Draws*]
              Tybalt, you rat-catcher, will you walk?
TYBALT   What wouldst thou have with me?
MERCUTIO   Good King of Cats, nothing but one of your nine lives
              that I mean to make bold withal, and as you shall use me
              hereafter, dry-beat the rest of the eight.

This stuff's all a bit <u>tricky</u> too.

<u>Don't</u> get <u>freaked out</u> if you don't understand <u>every</u> word.

...but Sometimes <u>Wider Knowledge</u> Will Help

All of the stuff about Mercutio calling Tybalt "rat-catcher" and "King of Cats" is really <u>odd</u>, unless you know where it comes from. In fact, Mercutio is <u>insulting</u> Tybalt's <u>name</u>.

Hey, Reynard!
Hey, Tibalt!

That's a <u>great point</u> to make about <u>how</u> the scene becomes <u>more tense</u> — but <u>only</u> if you've <u>got</u> the wider knowledge in the first place. The insult comes from the name of a cat in a popular story in Shakespeare's time — see Section Four.

If you've got <u>wider knowledge</u> then <u>use</u> it — but <u>only</u> if it's <u>relevant</u> to the task.

Facts about fat people — that's wider knowledge...

There's <u>no need</u> to understand <u>every single word</u> — if you don't get something, <u>move on</u> until you find the next bit that is <u>relevant</u> to the question. But if you do have <u>wider knowledge</u>, use it.

Section Eight — Writing About The Mood

Planning Your Answer

Planning an answer to a mood question is fairly straightforward — use the hints to help you.

Use the Hints to Help Make a Plan

These are the things the examiners think it's important for you to talk about — so you'd be mad not to.

The Hint Fairies

In your answer pay particular attention to:

— the opening of the scene (lines 1-48);

— the interaction between Mercutio and Tybalt;

— Romeo's words and actions;

— the arrival of the Prince at the end.

Write Your Plan in Rough Notes

Don't forget — the idea of a plan is to make sure you know roughly what you're going to talk about. That way you won't run out of steam halfway through.

1. Opening scene — tense because they could get into a fight — Tybalt enters — more tension — Benvolio tries to calm them down.

2. Tybalt/Mercutio — T approaches them — M picks a fight — tense — T tries to provoke R — M won't give up — draws sword, exciting — they fight.

3. Romeo — tension, as expected to fight but tries to be nice — exciting, as mistakenly lets T kill M — torn between love and revenge — kills T — flees.

4. Prince — tense when B says P will "doom" R — B and Lady C debate what P should do — excitement as P suprisingly exiles R — sets up rest of play.

The notes shouldn't be very long.

My notes. All mine. Not for you.

Sigh

They don't need to be in proper sentences — no one but you will see them.

Save time by using shorthand — "T" for Tybalt, and so on. Just make sure you can understand what you write.

Sandpaper piano keys — they're rough notes...

Make sure you use the hints that the question gives you to plan your answer. Do your plan in note form, and use shorthand if you like. All that matters is that you can make sense of it.

Following Your Plan

It's no good having a great plan if you don't have time to write about half of it.

Write About Every Point in the Plan

Your plan is there to help you — if you've written a good one, then you need to make sure you get all the points in.

Time your answer to give yourself a chance to get them in.

Stick to the Plan as You Write Your Answer

Look at the notes you've made, and expand on each of them in turn.
Here's how you might turn point 1 of your plan into the opening part of your answer:

Use the words of the task to show the examiner you're focussed on it.

Shakespeare makes the scene tense right from the very first speech. Benvolio says they should go. If they stay they're sure to get into a fight — "if we meet we shall not scape a brawl" (line 3).

Erm... when I said "stick to the plan"...

Shakespeare adds to our impression that there will be a fight by having Mercutio tease Benvolio about how hot-headed he is (lines 5-29). All of the conversation between Benvolio and Mercutio is about quarrelling, so right from the start we expect a fight.

Mercutio and Benvolio's long conversation is only relevant because it tells us Mercutio is really up for a fight. The details aren't relevant — you don't need to write about them.

Don't leave anything out

Then Tybalt arrives and Mercutio faces up to him, adding to the tension. Benvolio tries to persuade Mercutio to back down, but Mercutio says, "I will not budge" (line 48). A fight looks more and more likely, and everything is happening faster.

I've skipped a chunk of dialogue between Mercutio and Tybalt here (lines 32-42). That's because I'm going to cover it in the second point of the plan.

Benvolio needs a sunhat — he'd be less hot-headed...

Keep an eye on the time. You don't have to divide your time exactly down to the last minute — just bear in mind how many points you have left to write about, and how much time has gone.

Writing A Clear Answer

The examiners like to <u>know</u> that you've planned your answer properly and taken note of the <u>hints</u> in the question — so don't be <u>shy</u> about telling them.

Remember to Link Up Your Points

A <u>good way</u> of linking your points is by <u>comparing</u> the bit you've just <u>finished talking about</u> with the <u>next bit</u> you're <u>about to look at</u>.

...makes the audience very tense.
    While the conversation between Benvolio and Mercutio creates some tension, the moment when Tybalt appears makes the scene much more exciting. Now it's time for action, not words.
    As soon as Tybalt enters...

You're <u>moving</u> from a point about <u>tension</u> to one about <u>excitement</u>.

Don't Wander Away from the Task

You'll <u>lose marks</u> for only <u>telling the story</u>. Write about <u>why</u> it's tense and exciting.

Don't forget to write in <u>paragraphs</u>.

This starts by explaining <u>which part</u> of the scene it's about.

Then it explains <u>why</u> it makes us tense or excited.

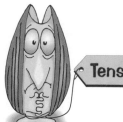

Tense Tim

As soon as Tybalt enters, Mercutio is clearly spoiling for a fight. Tybalt greets them in a civil enough way — "Gentlemen, good den" (line 33) — but Mercutio immediately tries to provoke him into fighting — "make it a word and a blow" (line 35). Tybalt rises to the bait and they trade insults.
    When Mercutio was only talking about quarrelling with Benvolio, the mood was quite tense. Now that Tybalt is onstage, it really looks like there will be a fight at any second. That's pretty exciting stuff.

On stage, the actors playing Tybalt and Mercutio would be squaring up with each other like boxers in a ring. They'd be in each others' faces, insulting each other. Then in line 67, Mercutio would have his sword out, waving it at Tybalt. Eight lines later Tybalt gets his sword out too. This would all look very exciting indeed.

Always think how the scene would look <u>onstage</u>. The words on the page only tell <u>half</u> the story.

Excitable John

Feeling tense — you're not past the worst...

Keep drumming it into the examiners that you've taken note of the task and you're doing your <u>best</u> to <u>answer</u> it. You have to <u>explain</u> what's happening in a way that makes it <u>relevant</u> to the task.

Using The Whole Play

Just because the question is about Act 3 Scene 1, it doesn't mean you can't bring in wider knowledge about what happens in the rest of the play — and about where the play is set.

You Can Use Other Bits of the Play

Knowing this helps you to explain what happens in Act 3 Scene 1.

...We know from Act 2 that Tybalt really wants to fight Romeo, not Mercutio. When Romeo arrives, Tybalt tries to leave Mercutio alone and turn his attention to Romeo — "peace be with you, sir, here comes my man" (line 49).

But I've got to fight Romeo - it says so in Act 2!

This tells you why the scene gets more exciting when Romeo appears — Tybalt's been looking for him so they can fight. But Romeo doesn't know this...

Background Knowledge Looks Good

This is all about explaining what's going on too.

Chicken!

When Romeo arrives, everyone is expecting him to fight. When he says instead that the name Capulet is as dear to him as his own, it amazes them all, and adds to the excitement of the scene. Mercutio is stunned, and calls it "dishonourable" — honour was very important in those days.

Instead of just saying, "Romeo refuses to fight", you need to say why he won't fight Tybalt.

Family ties were important too though. Romeo is now Tybalt's cousin by marriage. He would be wrong to fight Tybalt and he is dishonourable if he doesn't. This creates tension because the audience doesn't know what Romeo will decide to do.

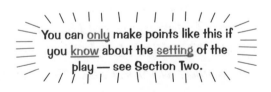

You can only make points like this if you know about the setting of the play — see Section Two.

Don't fall out of your mind — there's no-ledge there...

You can't get top marks by talking about the scene as if the rest of the play doesn't exist. You'll do much better if you bring in your knowledge of the rest of the play and the setting.

Proving Your Points

Examiners love it when you use <u>lots of quotes</u> from the scene. They show that you've read it and you <u>know what's going on</u>. If you can, try to put <u>at least one</u> quote in <u>every paragraph</u>.

You Need to Stick in Lots of Quotes

After the excitement of the fights, the focus swings back to tension again when the Prince gets involved. Benvolio alerts us to this by telling Romeo to run away before the Prince gets there or he'll be sentenced to death — "the Prince will doom thee death if thou art taken" (lines 125-126).

When the quote you're using is a bit <u>complicated</u>, it's a good idea to <u>explain</u> it to show you <u>understand</u> what it means.

<u>Don't</u> make your quotes <u>too long</u>. They only need to be a <u>few words</u>.

When the bit you're quoting is <u>easy to understand</u>, there's <u>no need</u> to explain it — just stick it in.

Benvolio and Montague both plead for Romeo's life to be spared, but Lady Capulet says, "Romeo must not live" (line 172)...

Keep On Answering the Task

...It's a bit like a courtroom scene, which makes us very tense because we are listening to the arguments and waiting to see whether the Prince will really sentence Romeo to death.

Stick loads of quotes in your answer.

Keep referring to the task, and explain <u>how</u> the scene is made <u>tense</u> and <u>exciting</u>.

I wish I didn't have to keep looking at you.

The Question

When the Prince announces "immediately we do exile him hence" (line 178), it is a big surprise — all the signs up till then were that he would give Romeo the death penalty. This is exciting, because you suddenly realise that Romeo and Juliet won't be able to see each other. Everything has gone wrong.

Give plenty of examples — meet your quota...

Quotes are important — examiners <u>love them</u>, so make sure you stick plenty in. Remember they <u>don't</u> need to be <u>long</u> to be useful. And don't forget to keep <u>answering</u> the question properly.

Finishing Your Answer

Make sure your answer ends on a <u>high note</u>. Trailing off looks like you <u>ran out</u> of ideas or <u>couldn't be bothered</u>. A decent final paragraph'll make your <u>whole answer</u> look loads better.

Remember to Make Time for Your Ending

You should keep looking at your watch or a clock while you write your answer, so you know when to <u>move on</u> to the next point — and when to start writing your <u>ending</u>.

1) Ideally leave about <u>five minutes</u> for writing your ending.

Look at me! Look at me!

2) If you <u>don't</u> have that much time, <u>don't worry</u>. A <u>one sentence</u> final paragraph beats <u>no</u> final paragraph by miles.

3) Make the final paragraph a <u>simple answer</u> to the question.

This is Your Last Chance to Answer the Question

Don't just stop writing — you have to <u>tie up</u> your answer clearly.

Use the <u>exact words</u> of the task to start the paragraph. That way you just can't help <u>sticking to the point</u>.

In your answer you talked about different parts of the scene separately. In your <u>last paragraph</u> try to say something which <u>sums up</u> the scene <u>overall</u>.

Shakespeare makes Act 3 Scene 1 tense and exciting by making the audience expect something bad to happen — creating tension — and then surprising them with different events. One of the biggest surprises is at the end of the scene when the Prince exiles Romeo. It means the whole scene ends on a tense and exciting note as the audience wonder what could happen next.

Sum up your answer in the last paragraph.

Excitement Tension Surprise + ??????

This final paragraph ends by mentioning the <u>overall effect</u> of the scene on the <u>audience</u>.

Finnish? — I come from Shveden...

Make sure you leave <u>time</u> to write a <u>good ending</u>. <u>Four or five minutes</u> should do the trick. It <u>impresses</u> the examiners, and it shows you've really tried to <u>do</u> what the task told you to.

Revision Summary

That's writing about the mood of a scene all taped up and ready to go. Only one more lot of revision questions to get your head round, and you'll be ready for anything — well, ready for your Shakespeare SAT at least.

1) For tasks about the mood of a scene you have to write about two things — what are they?

2) Why is it important to look at the stage directions when you read the scene?

3) Should you pay attention to what characters <u>don't</u> say?

4) Does the way people <u>talk</u> affect the way a scene makes you <u>feel</u>?

5) Will imagining how the scene looks on stage help you to answer mood questions?

6) Do the examiners expect you to understand every single word no matter how strange, old-fashioned and complicated it is?

7) In your SAT do you write about: a) car parks?   b) relevant bits of the scene only?

     c) the spaces between the lines?

8) Why should you use wider knowledge?

9) Is it a good idea to completely ignore the examiners' handy hints?

10) Should you use your best handwriting to write your notes?

11) Would you try to write about all the points in your plan?

12) What's a good way of linking one paragraph to the next?

13) Do the examiners give points for wandering away from the task?

14) Can you use what you know about other scenes from the play in your SAT?

15) How long should a quote usually be?

16) What's a good amount of time to leave for writing your ending?

What's <u>your</u> scene..?

Act 1, Scene 5
This is the scene where Romeo and Juliet first meet — at a party in Capulet's house.

ACT 1 SCENE 5

THE GREAT HALL IN CAPULET'S MANSION

SERVINGMEN come forth with napkins.

FIRST SERVINGMAN Where's Potpan, that he helps not to take away?
He shift a trencher? He scrape a trencher?

SECOND SERVINGMAN When good manners shall lie all in one or two
men's hands, and they unwashed too, 'tis a foul thing.

FIRST SERVINGMAN Away with the join-stools, remove the court-
cupboard, look to the plate. Good thou, save me a piece of
marchpane, and as thou loves me, let the porter let in Susan
Grindstone and Nell.

[Exit Second Servingman]

Anthony and Potpan!

[Enter two more SERVINGMEN]

THIRD SERVINGMAN Ay, boy, ready.

FIRST SERVINGMAN You are looked for and called for, asked for and
sought for, in the great chamber.

FOURTH SERVINGMAN We cannot be here and there too. Cheerly,
boys, be brisk a while, and the longer liver take all.

[They retire behind]

Enter CAPULET, LADY CAPULET, JULIET, TYBALT and his PAGE,
NURSE, and all the GUESTS and GENTLEWOMEN to the Maskers.

CAPULET Welcome, gentlemen! Ladies that have their toes
Unplagued with corns will walk a bout with you.
Ah, my mistresses, which of you all
Will now deny to dance? She that makes dainty,
She I'll swear hath corns. Am I come near ye now?
Welcome, gentlemen! I have seen the day
That I have worn a visor and could tell
A whispering tale in a fair lady's ear,
Such as would please; 'tis gone, 'tis gone, 'tis gone.
You are welcome, gentlemen. Come, musicians, play.

Music plays.

A hall, a hall, give room! and foot it, girls.

And they dance.

More light, you knaves, and turn the tables up;
And quench the fire, the room is grown too hot.
Ah, sirrah, this unlooked-for sport comes well.
Nay, sit, nay, sit, good Cousin Capulet,
For you and I are past our dancing days.
How long is't now since last yourself and I
Were in a mask?

COUSIN CAPULET   By'r lady, thirty years.

CAPULET What, man, 'tis not so much, 'tis not so much:
'Tis since the nuptial of Lucentio,
Come Pentecost as quickly as it will,
Some five and twenty years, and then we masked.

COUSIN CAPULET 'Tis more, 'tis more, his son is elder, sir;
His son is thirty.

CAPULET   Will you tell me that?
His son was but a ward two years ago.

ROMEO *[To a Servingman]* What lady's that which doth enrich the
hand
Of yonder knight?

SERVINGMAN I know not, sir.

ROMEO O she doth teach the torches to burn bright!
It seems she hangs upon the cheek of night
As a rich jewel in an Ethiop's ear -
Beauty too rich for use, for earth too dear:
So shows a snowy dove trooping with crows,
As yonder lady o'er her fellows shows.
The measure done, I'll watch her place of stand,
And touching hers, make blessed my rude hand.
Did my heart love till now? Forswear it, sight!
For I ne'er saw true beauty till this night.

TYBALT This, by his voice, should be a Montague.
Fetch me my rapier, boy.

[Exit Page]

What dares the slave
Come hither, covered with an antic face,
To fleer and scorn at our solemnity?
Now by the stock and honour of my kin,
To strike him dead I hold it not a sin.

CAPULET Why, how now, kinsman, wherefore storm you so?

TYBALT Uncle, this is a Montague, our foe:
A villain that is hither come in spite,
To scorn at our solemnity this night.

CAPULET Young Romeo is it?

TYBALT   'Tis he, that villain Romeo.

CAPULET Content thee, gentle coz, let him alone,
'A bears him like a portly gentleman;
And to say truth, Verona brags of him
To be a virtuous and well-governed youth.
I would not for the wealth of all this town
Here in my house do him disparagement;
Therefore be patient, take no note of him;
It is my will, the which if thou respect,

Line references: 5, 10, 15, 20, 25, 30, 35, 40, 45, 50, 55, 60, 65, 70

Phoarrrrrr! She's a babe!! ...but who's that guy with the big nose? — ROMEO'S MASK

Annotations:

(2) "trencher" = wooden plate

(5-6) = Take away the stools and sideboard and take care of the silver.

(7) "marchpane" = marzipan

(14) = the survivor takes all (winner takes all).

(16) = have a dance

(18-19) = If any woman refuses to dance, I'll say she's got corns. Does that hit the mark?

(25) = make room

(27) "quench" = put out

(28) "sirrah" = sir

(32) He means a masked dance.

(32) = By our lady

(34-36) = It's not so long — 25 years ago come Pentecost we danced at Lucentio's wedding.

(39) = underage, not an adult

(46-48) = She shows a beauty over other women too rich to use and too dear for the earth, like a white dove in a flock of crows.

(49) "measure" = dance

(54) = sword

(55) = horrible mask

(56) "fleer" = mock

(57-58) = By my family's honour it wouldn't be wrong to kill him.

(62) = festivities

(64) "coz" = cousin (or any relative)

(65) = He's acting like a well-mannered person

(68-69) = I wouldn't do him any harm here in my house for all the money in this town.

Annotations (top)

(109) = *methodically*

(110) = *wants*

(114) = *with*

(115-116) = *Whoever ends up with her will be rich.*

(117) = *in my enemy's power*

(118) = *The best fun's over.*

(121) = *refreshments*

(122) "e'en" = *even*

(125) "fay" = *faith*, "waxes" = *turns*

(127) "yond" = *that*

Oh rats.

He's a Montague.

(134) = *I'll die unmarried.*

(139) "prodigious" = *worrying/ominous*

(141) "'tis" = *this*

(142) = *right away/coming*

Play text (right column)

JULIET   You kiss by th'book.

NURSE Madam, your mother craves a word with you.

ROMEO What is her mother?

NURSE   Marry, bachelor,
Her mother is the lady of the house,
And a good lady, and a wise and virtuous.
I nursed her daughter that you talked withal;
I tell you, he that can lay hold of her
Shall have the chinks.

ROMEO   Is she a Capulet?
O dear account! my life is my foe's debt.

BENVOLIO Away, be gone, the sport is at the best.

ROMEO Ay, so I fear, the more is my unrest.

CAPULET Nay, gentlemen, prepare not to be gone,
We have a trifling foolish banquet towards.
                    [They whisper in his ear.]
Is it e'en so? Why then I thank you all.
I thank you, honest gentlemen, good night.
More torches here! Come on, then let's to bed.
Ah, sirrah, by my fay, it waxes late,
I'll to my rest.
                    [Exeunt all but Juliet and Nurse]

JULIET Come hither, Nurse. What is yond gentleman?

NURSE The son and heir of old Tiberio.

JULIET What's he that now is going out of door?

NURSE Marry, that I think be young Petruchio.

JULIET What's he that follows here, that would not dance?

NURSE I know not.

JULIET Go ask his name. If he be married,
My grave is like to be my wedding bed.

NURSE His name is Romeo, and a Montague,
The only son of your great enemy.

JULIET My only love sprung from my only hate!
Too early seen unknown, and known too late!
Prodigious birth of love it is to me,
That I must love a loathèd enemy.

NURSE What's tis? what's tis?

JULIET   A rhyme I learnt even now
Of one I danced withal.
                    One calls within, 'Juliet!'

NURSE Anon, anon!
Come let's away, the strangers all are gone.

Exeunt

Line numbers: 110, 115, 120, 125, 130, 135, 140

Play text (left column)

Show a fair presence, and put off these frowns,
An ill-beseeming semblance for a feast.

TYBALT It fits when such a villain is a guest:
I'll not endure him.

CAPULET   He shall be endured.
What, goodman boy, I say he shall, go to!
Am I the master here, or you ? Go to!
You'll not endure him? God shall mend my soul,
You'll make a mutiny among my guests!
You will set cock-a-hoop! you'll be the man!

TYBALT Why, uncle, 'tis a shame.

CAPULET   Go to, go to,
You are a saucy boy. Is't so indeed?
This trick may chance to scathe you, I know what.
You must contrary me! Marry, 'tis time. -
Well said, my hearts! - You are a princox, go,
Be quiet, or - More light, more light! - For shame,
I'll make you quiet, what! - Cheerly, my hearts!

TYBALT Patience perforce with wilful choler meeting
Makes my flesh tremble in their different greeting:
I will withdraw, but this intrusion shall,
Now seeming sweet, convert to bitt'rest gall.
                    Exit

ROMEO [*To Juliet*] If I profane with my unworthiest hand
This holy shrine, the gentle sin is this,
My lips, two blushing pilgrims, ready stand
To smooth that rough touch with a tender kiss.

JULIET Good pilgrim, you do wrong your hand too much,
Which mannerly devotion shows in this:
For saints have hands that pilgrims' hands do touch,
And palm to palm is holy palmers' kiss.

ROMEO Have not saints lips, and holy palmers too?

JULIET Ay, pilgrim, lips that they must use in prayer.

ROMEO O then, dear saint, let lips do what hands do:
They pray — grant thou, lest faith turn to despair.

JULIET Saints do not move, though grant for prayers' sake.

ROMEO Then move not while my prayer's effect I take.
                    [Kissing her.]
Thus from my lips, by thine, my sin is purged.

JULIET Then have my lips the sin that they have took.
                    [Kissing her again.]

ROMEO Sin from my lips? O trespass sweetly urged!
Give me my sin again.

Line numbers: 75, 80, 85, 90, *Exit*, 95, 100, 105

Annotations (left/bottom)

(72-74) = *Look happy and stop frowning — it's the wrong expression for a party.*

(74) = *I won't accept him.*

(76) = *less than a gentleman (= insult)*

(79) = *start a fight*

(80) = *You'll cause chaos.*

(81) = *insult*

(82) = *rude*

(83-84) = *This foolish behaviour could harm you; don't I know it. You go against my will. Well, it's time to teach you a lesson.*

(85) "princox" = *insolent boy*

(88-89) = *I'm shaking because my anger has to meet with patience against my will.*

(92-95) = *If I insult the shrine of your hand with my unworthy hand, then my sin is that my lips are ready to kiss it better.*

(96-99) = *Pilgrim, your touch wasn't rough, which shows proper devotion; pilgrims touch saints' hands, which is a proper "pilgrim's kiss".*

(103) = *My lips pray — grant them a kiss.*

(104) = *Saints don't do things, they just grant prayers.*

(106) = *My sin is taken away from my lips by yours.*

(107) = *Now my lips have got the sin on them.*

(109) = *I'll take my sin back.*

Section Nine — The Most Important Scenes

92

Notes (left):

Act 2, Scene 2
Romeo sneaks into Capulet's garden — he wants to see Juliet and speak to her again.

(1) = Only someone who's never been wounded makes jokes about scars.

(6) = That you, her servant, are more beautiful than she is.

(8) = Her virgin's appearance is sick and green, and only fools wear that look; throw it off

(13) = talks 'to me

(15-17) = Her eyes could take the place of two of the most beautiful stars in heaven.

(18-19) = If those stars took the place of her eyes, her cheeks brightness would shame them.

(21) "stream" = shine

(29) = The eyes turned up so you can mainly see the whites.

ACT 2 SCENE 2
Capulet's orchard
ROMEO advances.

ROMEO He jests at scars that never felt a wound.
But soft, what light through yonder window breaks?
It is the east, and Juliet is the sun.
Arise, fair sun, and kill the envious moon,
Who is already sick and pale with grief   5
That thou, her maid, art far more fair than she.
Be not her maid, since she is envious;
Her vestal livery is but sick and green,
And none but fools do wear it; cast it off.
[JULIET *appears aloft as at a window.*]
It is my lady, O it is my love!   10
O that she knew she were!
She speaks, yet she says nothing; what of that?
Her eye discourses, I will answer it.
I am too bold, 'tis not to me she speaks:
Two of the fairest stars in all the heaven,   15
Having some business, do entreat her eyes
To twinkle in their spheres till they return.
What if her eyes were there, they in her head?
The brightness of her cheek would shame those stars,
As daylight doth a lamp; her eyes in heaven   20
Would through the airy region stream so bright
That birds would sing and think it were not night.
See how she leans her cheek upon her hand!
O that I were a glove upon that hand,
That I might touch that cheek!
JULIET   Ay me!
ROMEO [*Aside*]   She speaks.   25
O speak again, bright angel, for thou art
As glorious to this night, being o'er my head,
As is a wingèd messenger of heaven
Unto the white-upturnèd wondering eyes
Of mortals that fall back to gaze on him,   30
When he bestrides the lazy puffing clouds,
And sails upon the bosom of the air.

JULIET O Romeo, Romeo, wherefore art thou Romeo?
Deny thy father and refuse thy name;
Or if thou wilt not, be but sworn my love,
And I'll no longer be a Capulet.   35
ROMEO [*Aside*] Shall I hear more, or shall I speak at this?
JULIET 'Tis but thy name that is my enemy;
Thou art thyself, though not a Montague.
What's Montague? It is nor hand nor foot,
Nor arm nor face, nor any other part   40
Belonging to a man. O be some other name!
What's in a name? That which we call a rose
By any other word would smell as sweet;
So Romeo would, were he not Romeo called,
Retain that dear perfection which he owes   45
Without that title. Romeo, doff thy name,
And for thy name, which is no part of thee,
Take all myself.
ROMEO   I take thee at thy word:
Call me but love, and I'll be new baptised;
Henceforth I never will be Romeo.   50
JULIET What man art thou that thus bescreened in night
So stumblest on my counsel?
ROMEO   By a name
I know not how to tell thee who I am.
My name, dear saint, is hateful to myself,
Because it is an enemy to thee;
Had I it written, I would tear the word.   55
JULIET My ears have yet not drunk a hundred words
Of thy tongue's uttering, yet I know the sound.
Art thou not Romeo, and a Montague?
ROMEO Neither, fair maid, if either thee dislike.
JULIET How camest thou hither, tell me, and wherefore?   60
The orchard walls are high and hard to climb,
And the place death, considering who thou art,
If any of my kinsmen find thee here.
ROMEO With lovers light wings did I o'erperch these walls,
For stony limits cannot hold love out,   65
And what love can do, that dares love attempt:
Therefore thy kinsmen are no stop to me.

Notes (right):

(33) = Why are you Romeo?

(38-39) = Only your name is my enemy. You won't change yourself even if you change your name.

(43-44) = A rose would smell as nice even if it had a different name.

(47) "doff" = take off

(48-49) = and instead of your name take me.

[I baptise this child "Love".]

(52) = hidden

(53) = interrupts my private thoughts.

(53-56) = I don't know how to say who I am using a name. I hate it because it's your enemy's.

(58-59) = you haven't even said 100 words and I know who you are.

(62) = How did you get here and why?

(65) "kinsmen" = relatives

(66) = I flew over these walls with a lover's wings

(68) = Whatever love can do, it'll dare to try.

"You're not so bad yourself, chuck!"

"Are you going to tell me you love me?"

"Oi! Romeo! You're ace!"

JULIET If they do see thee, they will murder thee. (70)
ROMEO Alack, there lies more peril in thine eye
Than twenty of their swords. Look thou but sweet,
And I am proof against their enmity.
JULIET I would not for the world they saw thee here.
ROMEO I have night's cloak to hide me from their eyes, (75)
And but thou love me, let them find me here;
My life were better ended by their hate,
Than death prorogued, wanting of thy love.
JULIET By whose direction found'st thou out this place?
ROMEO By Love, that first did prompt me to enquire: (80)
He lent me counsel, and I lent him eyes.
I am no pilot, yet wert thou as far
As that vast shore washed with the farthest sea,
I should adventure for such merchandise.
JULIET Thou knowest the mask of night is on my face, (85)
Else would a maiden blush bepaint my cheek
For that which thou hast heard me speak tonight.
Fain would I dwell on form, fain, fain deny
What I have spoke, but farewell compliment.
Dost thou love me? I know thou wilt say 'Ay'; (90)
And I will take thy word; yet if thou swear'st,
Thou mayst prove false: at lovers' perjuries
They say Jove laughs. O gentle Romeo,
If thou dost love, pronounce it faithfully;
Or if thou think'st I am too quickly won, (95)
I'll frown and be perverse, and say thee nay,
So thou wilt woo, but else not for the world.
In truth, fair Montague, I am too fond,
And therefore thou mayst think my behaviour light:
But trust me, gentleman, I'll prove more true (100)
Than those that have more coying to be strange.
I should have been more strange, I must confess,
But that thou overheard'st, ere I was ware,
My true-love passion; therefore pardon me,
And not impute this yielding to light love, (105)
Which the dark night hath so discoverèd.

ROMEO Lady, by yonder blessèd moon I vow,
That tips with silver all these fruit-tree tops -
JULIET O swear not by the moon, th'inconstant moon,
That monthly changes in her circled orb, (110)
Lest that thy love prove likewise variable.
ROMEO What shall I swear by?
JULIET Do not swear at all;
Or if thou wilt, swear by thy gracious self,
Which is the god of my idolatry,
And I'll believe thee.
ROMEO If my heart's dear love - (115)
JULIET Well, do not swear. Although I joy in thee,
I have no joy of this contract tonight,
It is too rash, too unadvised, too sudden,
Too like the lightning, which doth cease to be
Ere one can say 'It lightens'. Sweet, good night: (120)
This bud of love, by summer's ripening breath,
May prove a beauteous flower when next we meet.
Good night, good night! as sweet repose and rest
Come to thy heart as that within my breast.
ROMEO O wilt thou leave me so unsatisfied? (125)
JULIET What satisfaction canst thou have tonight?
ROMEO Th'exchange of thy love's faithful vow for mine.
JULIET I gave thee mine before thou didst request it;
And yet I would it were to give again.
ROMEO Wouldst thou withdraw it? for what purpose, love? (130)
JULIET But to be frank and give it thee again,
And yet I wish but for the thing I have:
My bounty is as boundless as the sea,
My love as deep; the more I give to thee
The more I have, for both are infinite. (135)
[Nurse calls within.]
I hear some noise within; dear love, adieu! -
Anon, good Nurse! - Sweet Montague, be true.
Stay but a little, I will come again. [Exit above]
ROMEO O blessèd, blessèd night! I am afeard,
Being in night, all this is but a dream, (140)
Too flattering-sweet to be substantial.

Glossary / notes:

(71) "peril" = danger

(73) "proof" = armoured "enmity" = hatred

(76) = Unless you love me, let them find me here.

(77-78) = If I don't have your love, it'd be better if I were killed than my death put off.

(81) "counsel" = advice

(82-84) = I'm not a sailor, but even if you were as far away as the furthest away sea, I would risk the journey for you.

(86) = paint, colour

(88) = gladly

(89) = forget the normal rules

(92-93) = They say the god Jove laughs at lies told by lovers.

(95-97) = If you think I've given in too easily, I'll frown, get cross and say no, so you have to persuade me, otherwise I won't.

(98) = I'm too in love

(99) "light" = careless

(101) "coying" = skill at flirting, "strange" = aloof

(103) "ware" = aware

(104-105) = Therefore forgive me and don't think my surrender to you is careless love.

(111) "lest" = in case

(113) = having all the graces of body and spirit

(116-117) = Although you make me happy, I'm not happy about making these promises tonight.

(120-122) She's saying this is a good start but that's enough for now.

(123) = relaxation

(127) "vow" = promise

(129) = I wish I had my vow back to give it again.

(131) "frank" = generous

(133) "bounty" = generosity

(134-135) = The more love I give you, the more love I get back since both of them are endless amounts.

(136) = goodbye!

(138) "anon" = coming!

(139) = afraid

(140-141) = This is only a dream, too wonderful to be real.

ROMEO   Let me stand here till thou remember it.
JULIET   I shall forget, to have thee still stand there,
         Remembering how I love thy company.
ROMEO   And I'll still stay, to have thee still forget,
         Forgetting any other home but this.
JULIET   'Tis almost morning, I would have thee gone: 175
         And yet no farther than a wanton's bird,
         That lets it hop a little from his hand,
         Like a poor prisoner in his twisted gyves,
         And with a silken thread plucks it back again,   180
         So loving-jealous of his liberty.
ROMEO   I would I were thy bird.
JULIET   Sweet, so would I,
         Yet I should kill thee with much cherishing.
         Good night, good night! Parting is such sweet sorrow,   185
         That I shall say good night till it be morrow.
                                [Exit above]
ROMEO   Sleep dwell upon thine eyes, peace in thy breast!
         Would I were sleep and peace, so sweet to rest!
         Hence will I to my ghostly sire's close cell,
         His help to crave, and my dear hap to tell.
                                Exit

(172) = I'll forget, so that you'll always be there.

(174) = And I'll stay here, so you'll keep on forgetting.

(160-163) = I wish you were gone, but no further than a spoilt child's pet bird — the child lets it hop about like a prisoner in chains, but pulls it back with a silk thread tied on it, because he/she's jealous of it being free.

(183) = too much love

(188-189) = I'll go from here to my spiritual father's cell (ie Friar Lawrence's) to ask his help and tell him my good fortune.

What Shakespeare would've done if he hadn't written plays...

Just one last fight, and the world championship will be mine!

                 [Enter Juliet above.]
JULIET   Three words, dear Romeo, and good night indeed.
         If that thy bent of love be honourable,
         Thy purpose marriage, send me word tomorrow,   145
         By one that I'll procure to come to thee,
         Where and what time thou wilt perform the rite,
         And all my fortunes at thy foot I'll lay,
         And follow thee my lord throughout the world.
NURSE [Within] Madam!
JULIET I come, anon. - But if thou meanest not well,   150
         I do beseech thee -
NURSE [Within]   Madam!
JULIET   By and by I come -
         To cease thy strife, and leave me to my grief.
         Tomorrow will I send.
ROMEO   So thrive my soul -
JULIET   A thousand times good night!
                                [Exit above]
ROMEO   A thousand times the worse, to want thy light.   155
         Love goes toward love as schoolboys from their books,
         But love from love, toward school with heavy looks.
                                [Retiring slowly]
                    Enter Juliet again [above].
JULIET   Hist, Romeo, hist! O for a falc'ner's voice,
         To lure this tassel-gentle back again:
         Bondage is hoarse, and may not speak aloud,   160
         Else would I tear the cave where Echo lies,
         And make her airy tongue more hoarse than mine
         With repetition of my Romeo's name.
ROMEO   It is my soul that calls upon my name.
         How silver-sweet sound lovers' tongues by night,   165
         Like softest music to attending ears!
JULIET   Romeo!
ROMEO   My niësse?
JULIET   What o'clock tomorrow
         Shall I send to thee?
ROMEO   By the hour of nine.
JULIET   I will not fail, 'tis twenty year till then.
         I have forgot why I did call thee back.   170

(143) = If the intention of your love is honourable, and you want to marry me, send me a message tomorrow by someone I'll send to say where and when the ceremony will happen

See ya! I've gotta go!

(151) "beseech" = ask

(151 & 152) = I ask you... to stop this nonsense and leave me to my sadness.

(154) = prospers

(156-157) = Love goes to love like kids leaving school (happily): but it goes away from love like kids going to school

(158) "hist" is what a falconer (bird-keeper) says to the falcon.

(159) A 'tassel-gentle' is a kind of falcon only used by princes.

(160-163) = I have to keep quiet, or I would shout Romeo's name until it echoed.

(167) "niësse" = nesting hawk

See you at 9 o'clock tomorrow.

ACT 3 SCENE 1

Verona, a public place

Enter MERCUTIO *and his* PAGE, BENVOLIO, *and men.*

BENVOLIO I pray thee, good Mercutio, let's retire:
The day is hot, the Capels are abroad,
And if we meet we shall not scape a brawl,
For now, these hot days, is the mad blood stirring.

MERCUTIO Thou art like one of these fellows that, when he
enters the confines of a tavern, claps me his sword upon
the table, and says 'God send me no need of thee!'; and by 5
the operation of the second cup draws him on the drawer,
when indeed there is no need.

BENVOLIO Am I like such a fellow?

MERCUTIO Come, come, thou art as hot a Jack in thy mood as 10
any in Italy, and as soon moved to be moody, and as soon
moody to be moved.

BENVOLIO And what to?

MERCUTIO Nay, and there were two such, we should have 15
none shortly, for one would kill the other. Thou? why, thou
wilt quarrel with a man that hath a hair more or a hair less
in his beard than thou hast; thou wilt quarrel with a man for
cracking nuts, having no other reason but because thou
hast hazel eyes. What eye but such an eye would spy out 20
such a quarrel? Thy head is as full of quarrels as an egg is
full of meat, and yet thy head hath been beaten as addle as
an egg for quarrelling. Thou hast quarrelled with a man for
coughing in the street, because he hath wakened thy dog
that hath lain asleep in the sun. Didst thou not fall out with 25
a tailor for wearing his new doublet before Easter? with
another for tying his new shoes with old riband? and yet
thou wilt tutor me from quarrelling?

BENVOLIO And I were so apt to quarrel as thou art, any man
should buy the fee-simple of my life for an hour and a quarter. 30

MERCUTIO The fee-simple? O simple!

Enter TYBALT, PETRUCHIO, *and others.*

BENVOLIO By my head, here comes the Capulets.

MERCUTIO By my heel, I care not.

TYBALT Follow me close, for I will speak to them.
Gentlemen, *good den*, a word with one of you. 35

MERCUTIO And but one word with one of us? couple it with

something, make it a word and a blow.

TYBALT *You shall find me apt enough to that, sir, and you will
give me occasion.*

MERCUTIO Could you not take some occasion without giving? 40

TYBALT Mercutio, thou consortest with Romeo.

MERCUTIO Consort? what, dost thou make us minstrels? And
thou make minstrels of us, look to hear nothing but
discords. Here's my fiddlestick, here's that shall make you
dance. 'Zounds, consort! 45

BENVOLIO We talk here in the public haunt of men:
Either withdraw unto some private place,
Or reason coldly of your grievances,
Or else depart; here all eyes gaze on us. 50

MERCUTIO Men's eyes were made to look, and let them gaze;
I will not budge for no man's pleasure, I.

Enter ROMEO.

TYBALT Well, peace be with you, sir, *here comes my man.*

MERCUTIO But I'll be hanged, sir, if he wear your livery, 55
Marry, go before to field, he' ll be your follower;
Your worship in that sense may call him man.

TYBALT *Romeo, the love I bear thee can afford
No better term than this: thou art a villain.*

ROMEO Tybalt, the reason that I have to love thee 60
Doth much excuse the appertaining rage
To such a greeting. Villain am I none;
Therefore farewell, I see thou knowest me not.

TYBALT *Boy, this shall not excuse the injuries
That thou hast done me, therefore turn and draw.*

ROMEO I do protest I never injured thee, 65
But love thee better than thou canst devise,
Till thou shalt know the reason of my love;
And so, good Capulet, which name I tender
As dearly as mine own, be satisfied.

MERCUTIO O calm, dishonourable, vile submission! 70
'Alla stoccata' carries it away. [*Draws*]
Tybalt, you rat-catcher, will you walk?

TYBALT What wouldst thou have with me?

MERCUTIO Good King of Cats, nothing but one of your nine
lives that I mean to make bold withal, and as you shall use 75
me hereafter, dry-beat the rest of the eight. Will you pluck

Section Nine — The Most Important Scenes

Annotations:

Tybalt's looking for a fight with Romeo, who won't fight, so Mercutio fights Tybalt, and is killed. Romeo kills Tybalt in revenge, and the Prince banishes Romeo from Verona.

(1-4) = Mercutio, let's go home. The Capulets are about and if we meet some in this heat, we'll end up in a fight.

(5-9) = You're one of those people who say you don't want to get into a fight, but then goes and starts one.

(11) Moody = angry

(15-28) = If there were two of you, they'd end up killing each other. You'd fight a man for no reason.

No, I'm an egg not a quarrel. The guy doing the pictures mustav got confused!

(29-30) = If I was as quick to fight as you are, my life wouldn't be worth buying for an hour and a quarter (if someone has the fee-simple of something, it means they own it).

(32) = Oh dear

(33) = Doesn't bother me

(35) "Good den" = good evening

(38-39) = I will if you give me a reason

(40-41) = Can't you make a reason up without one from me.

(43) Mercutio's playing on the words: consort means to hang about with someone, but it's also a group of musicians. He means sword by fiddlestick, and zounds is a swear word.

(47-50) = everyone's watching us. Either be sensible, go somewhere private, or just give it up.

(53) = Here's the man I'm after.

(54-56) Mercutio's playing on words again. He is taking 'man' to mean servant or follower, and saying that the only way Romeo will follow Tybalt is if Tybalt is going to a fight.

(57-58) = I love you enough to say you're a villian.

(59-62) = I love you enough to excuse you for saying that. I'm not a villian so you can't really know me. Bye.

(63-64) = That doesn't make up for everything you've done before — so fight.

(65-69) = I never hurt you, I love you more than you can imagine until you know why. So be happy, cos I like your name as much as mine.

(71) Alla Stoccata is a sword-fighting word. Mercutio is saying he'll fight instead of Romeo.

(72-74) Yet again, Mercutio is playing on words. There's a story with a cat called Tibalt, so he's calling Tybalt rat-catcher and king of cats.

96

(109-110) = Hanging around Juliet must have made me weak and woman-like.

(114-120) = I won't be gentle any more. Take back what you said about me being a villian. Mercutio's dead and wants you to be too, to keep him company. One of us will die.

(125) = It's going to be you.

(127-130) = Romeo, get out of here. The Prince will have you executed if you stay.

I ain't nobody's fool man!

(130) The officer doesn't realise that Tybalt's dead, so he's asking him to get up.

With Tybalt's slander - Tybalt, that an hour
Hath been my cousin. O sweet Juliet,
Thy beauty hath made me effeminate,
And in my temper softened valour's steel!

Enter BENVOLIO

110

BENVOLIO O Romeo, Romeo, brave Mercutio is dead.
That gallant spirit hath aspired the clouds,
Which too untimely here did scorn the earth.
ROMEO This day's black fate on moe days doth depend,
This but begins the woe others must end.

15

[*Enter* TYBALT]

BENVOLIO Here comes the furious Tybalt back again.
ROMEO Again, in triumph, and Mercutio slain?
Away to heaven, respective lenity,
And fire-eyed fury be my conduct now!
Now, Tybalt, take the 'villain' back again
That late thou gavest me, for Mercutio's soul
Is but a little way above our heads,
Staying for thine to keep him company:
Either thou or I, or both, must go with him.

120

TYBALT *Thou wretched boy, that didst consort him here,*
Shalt with him hence.

ROMEO   This shall determine that.

They fight; Tybalt falls.

125

BENVOLIO Romeo, away, be gone!
The citizens are up, and Tybalt slain.
Stand not amazed, the Prince will doom thee death
If thou art taken. Hence be gone, away!
ROMEO O, I am fortune's fool.
BENVOLIO   Why dost thou stay?

130

Exit Romeo

Enter Citizens [*as* OFFICERS *of the Watch*]

OFFICER Which way ran he that killed Mercutio?
Tybalt, that murderer, which way ran he?
BENVOLIO There lies that Tybalt.
OFFICER   Up, sir, go with me;
I charge thee in the Prince's name obey.

135

---

your sword out of his pilcher by the ears? Make haste, lest
mine be about your ears ere it be out.
TYBALT I am for you. [*Drawing*]
ROMEO Gentle Mercutio, put thy rapier up.
MERCUTIO Come, sir, your 'passado'.

[*They fight*]

80

ROMEO Draw, Benvolio, beat down their weapons.
Gentlemen, for shame forbear this outrage!
Tybalt, Mercutio, the Prince expressly hath
Forbid this bandying in Verona streets.

[*Romeo steps between them*]

Hold, Tybalt! Good Mercutio!

[*Tybalt under Romeo's arm. thrusts Mercutio in*]

          Away Tybalt [*with his followers*]

MERCUTIO   I am hurt.
A plague a'both houses! I am sped.
Is he gone and hath nothing?

85

BENVOLIO   What, art thou hurt?
MERCUTIO Ay, ay, a scratch, a scratch, marry, 'tis enough.
Where is my page? Go, villain, fetch a surgeon.

[*Exit Page*]

ROMEO Courage, man, the hurt cannot be much.

90

MERCUTIO No, 'tis not so deep as a well, nor so wide as a
church-door, but 'tis enough, 'twill serve. Ask for me
tomorrow, and you shall find me a grave man. I am
peppered, I warrant, for this world. A plague a'both your
houses! 'Zounds, a dog, a rat, a mouse, a cat, to scratch a
man to death! A braggart, a rogue, a villain, that fights by
the book of arithmetic. Why the dev'l came you between
us? I was hurt under your arm.
ROMEO I thought all for the best.

95

MERCUTIO Help me into some house, Benvolio,
Or I shall faint. A plague a'both your houses!
They have made worms' meat of me. I have it
And soundly too. Your houses!

100

Exit [*with Benvolio*]

ROMEO This gentleman, the Princess near ally,
My very friend, hath got this mortal hurt
In my behalf; my reputation stained

105

---

(79) = Don't do it!

(80) "passado" = sword thrusts

(81-84) = Benvolio, get your sword out and help me stop them. The Prince has forbidden fighting in the streets

This is terrible. Romeo steps between Tybalt and Mercutio to stop them, and Tybalt stabs Mercutio under Romeo's arm.

(85-86) = Damn Caplets and Montagues. I'm injured.

(89-90) = Even dying, Mercutio is playing with words. He's saying tomorrow he'll be dead (in his grave), but also playing on grave meaning serious.

(99) = I was trying to help.

(102-103) = I've had it, that's for sure.

Zounds!

(104-108) = My friend, who was related to the Prince, has been killed in my place, by Tybalt, who's now my cousin.

Section Nine — The Most Important Scenes

(173-174) = Romeo killed Tybalt, but Tybalt had killed Mercutio. Who should pay the price?

(175-177) = Not Romeo. He only did what the law should have done.

(181-190) = For that, he's banished. I'm watching your squabble — it's killed a relative of mine. I'll fine you heavily so you'll all suffer as I do. I won't listen to you complain, so don't bother trying. Romeo should get out of here, or he'll be killed.

(191-192) = Get the body out of here. If I was merciful to murderers, it would be encouraging them.

Enter PRINCE, old MONTAGUE, CAPULET, *their* WIVES, *and all.*
PRINCE Where are the vile beginners of this fray?
BENVOLIO O noble Prince, I can discover all
The unlucky manage of this fatal brawl;
There lies the man, slain by young Romeo,
That slew thy kinsman, brave Mercutio. 140
LADY CAPULET Tybalt, my cousin! O my brother's child!
O Prince! O husband! O, the blood is spilled
Of my dear kinsman. Prince, as thou art true,
For blood of ours, shed blood of Montague.
O cousin, cousin! 145
PRINCE Benvolio, who began this bloody fray?
BENVOLIO Tybalt, here slain, whom Romeo's hand did slay.
Romeo, that spoke him fair, bid him bethink
How nice the quarrel was, and urged withal
Your high displeasure; all this, uttered 150
With gentle breath, calm look, knees humbly bowed,
Could not take truce with the unruly spleen
Of Tybalt deaf to peace, but that he tilts
With piercing steel at bold Mercutio's breast,
Who, all as hot, turns deadly point to point, 155
And with a martial scorn, with one hand beats
Cold death aside, and with the other sends
It back to Tybalt, whose dexterity
Retorts it. Romeo he cries aloud,
'Hold, friends! friends, part!' and swifter than his tongue, 160
His agile arm beats down their fatal points,
And 'twixt them rushes; underneath whose arm
An envious thrust from Tybalt hit the life
Of stout Mercutio, and then Tybalt fled;
But by and by comes back to Romeo, 165
Who had but newly entertained revenge,
And to't they go like lightning, for, ere I
Could draw to part them, was stout Tybalt slain;
And as he fell, did Romeo turn and fly.
This is the truth, or let Benvolio die. 170
LADY CAPULET He is a kinsman to the Montague,
Affection makes him false, he speaks not true:
Some twenty of them fought in this black strife,
And all those twenty could but kill one life.
I beg for justice, which thou, Prince, must give : 175
Romeo slew Tybalt, Romeo must not live.

PRINCE Romeo slew him, he slew Mercutio;
Who now the price of his dear blood doth owe?
MONTAGUE Not Romeo, Prince, he was Mercutio's friend;
His fault concludes but what the law should end, 180
The life of Tybalt.
PRINCE   And for that offence
Immediately we do exile him hence.
I have an interest in your hearts' proceeding
My blood for your rude brawls doth lie a-bleeding;
But I'll amerce you with so strong a fine 185
That you shall all repent the loss of mine.
I will be deaf to pleading and excuses,
Nor tears nor prayers shall purchase out abuses:
Therefore use none. Let Romeo hence in haste,
Else, when he is found, that hour is his last. 190
Bear hence this body, and attend our will:
Mercy but murders, pardoning those that kill.

Exeunt

(136) = Where are the people who started it?

(137-140) = I can tell you everything. On the floor is Tybalt, who killed Mercutio and was then killed by Romeo.

(143-144) = Prince, kill Romeo in return for this.

(146-169) = Tybalt started it. Romeo asked him not to, 'cos he knew you wouldn't like it, but Tybalt fought anyway. Romeo tried to stop them and got in the way, then Tybalt stabbed Mercutio under Romeo's arm. Tybalt ran away but came back, and Romeo killed him before I could stop them. Then Romeo ran off.

(171-176) = He's part of Romeo's family — he's lying. There were twenty of them, and they still only just managed to kill Tybalt. Romeo must be executed for killing Tybalt.

Well that's it. I've had it with you lot. You can all sling yer hooks as far as I'm concerned. Go on — beat it!

Section Nine — The Most Important Scenes

98

ACT 3 SCENE 2

Juliet's room in Capulet's mansion

Enter JULIET alone.

JULIET Gallop apace, you fiery-footed steeds,
Towards **Phoebus'** lodging; such a waggoner
As Phaeton would whip you to the west,
And bring in cloudy night immediately.
Spread thy close curtain, love-performing Night, 5
That runaways' eyes may wink, and Romeo
Leap to these arms, untalked of and unseen:
Lovers can see to do their amorous rites
By their own beauties, or if love be blind,
It best agrees with night. Come, civil Night, 10
Thou sober-suited matron all in black,
And learn me how to lose a winning match,
Played for a pair of stainless maidenhoods.
Hood my unmanned blood, bating in my cheeks,
With thy black mantle, till strange love grow bold, 15
Think true love acted simple modesty.
Come, Night, come, Romeo, come, thou day in night,
For thou wilt lie upon the wings of night,
Whiter than new snow upon a raven's back.
Come, gentle Night, come, loving, black-browed Night, 20
Give me my Romeo, and when I shall die,
Take him and cut him out in little stars,
And he will make the face of heaven so fine
That all the world will be in love with night,
And pay no worship to the garish sun. 25
O, I have bought the mansion of a love,
But not possessed it, and though I am sold,
Not yet enjoyed. So tedious is this day
As is the night before some festival
To an impatient child that hath new robes 30
And may not wear them. O, here comes my Nurse,

Enter NURSE, with [*the ladder of cords* [*in her lap*].

And she brings news, and every tongue that speaks
But Romeo's name speaks heavenly eloquence.
Now, Nurse, what news? What hast thou there? The cords
That Romeo bid thee fetch? 35

NURSE   Ay, ay, the cords.

[*Throws them down*]

JULIET Ay me, what news? Why dost thou wring thy hands?
NURSE Ah weraday, he's dead, he's dead, he's dead!
We are undone, lady, we are undone.
Alack the day, he's gone, he's killed, he's dead!
JULIET Can heaven be so envious?
NURSE   Romeo can, 40
Though heaven cannot. O Romeo, Romeo!
Who ever would have thought it? Romeo!
JULIET What devil art thou that dost torment me thus?
This torture should be roared in dismal hell.
Hath Romeo slain himself? Say thou but 'ay 45
And that bare vowel 'I' shall poison more
Than the death-darting eye of cockatrice.
I am not I, if there be such an 'ay',
Or those eyes shut, that makes thee answer 'ay'.
If he be slain, say 'ay', or if not, 'no': 50
Brief sounds determine my weal or woe.
NURSE I saw the wound, I saw it with mine eyes
(God save the mark!), here on his manly breast:
A piteous corse, a bloody piteous corse,
Pale, pale as ashes, all bedaubed in blood, 55
All in gore blood; I sounded at the sight.
JULIET O break, my heart, poor bankrout, break at once!
To prison, eyes, ne'er look on liberty!
Vile earth, to earth resign, end motion here,
And thou and Romeo press one heavy bier! 60
NURSE O Tybalt, Tybalt, the best friend I had!
O courteous Tybalt, honest gentleman,
That ever I should live to see thee dead!
JULIET What storm is this that blows so contrary?
Is Romeo slaughtered? and is Tybalt dead? 65
My dearest cousin, and my dearer lord?
Then, dreadful trumpet, sound the general doom,
For who is living, if those two are gone?
NURSE Tybalt is gone and Romeo banishèd,
Romeo that killed him, he is banished. 70
JULIET O God, did Romeo's hand shed Tybalt's blood?
NURSE It did, it did, alas the day, it did!

Section Nine — The Most Important Scenes

Act 3, Scene 2 The Nurse tells Juliet that Romeo has killed Tybalt, and Romeo has been banished from Verona. Juliet's dead upset, but the Nurse says Romeo will still come to see her tonight.

(1-2) = *I want the sun to go down.*

(2-3) *Phoebus* is a sun god, and Phaeton is his son.

(13) "maidenhood" = virginity

(10-14) = *May dark night teach me how to win Romeo by surrendering to him, and hide my blushing cheeks.*

(1-30) Juliet's just saying that she wishes it would be nighttime more quickly, because that's when Romeo's coming to see her.

(26-28) She's saying that by marrying Romeo, they have the right to enjoy each other's bodies, but they haven't yet.

(32-33) = *every tongue that speaks nothing but Romeo's name, speaks something really nice.*

(34 & 35) "the cords" = rope ladder

Oooh, I just had to buy it. Half price at Woolworths. And isn't it adorable!

(37) "undone" = ruined

(38-51) The Nurse is upset because Tybalt's dead. Juliet's confused because it sounds like the Nurse means Romeo's dead, and that he killed himself.

(40) "envious" = nasty

(43-47) = *Why are you tormenting me like this? Has Romeo killed himself? Just say "yes", and that word will poison me more than a cockatrice would (a mythical beast).*

(45) "ay" = yes

(51) = *Short words determine my happiness or misery.*

(54) "corse" = corpse

(55-56) = *covered in clotted blood; I fainted at the sight.*

(57-60) = *Let me die too and join Romeo on the funeral bed.*

(64) = *What's this terrible situation?*

(66) "dearer lord" = she means Romeo

(69-72) Now the Nurse explains that Romeo killed Tybalt, and has been banished (he has to leave the city).

(73-79) Juliet's talking about how Romeo's a nice bloke, but he's done a terrible thing. These images are all opposites, for example a raven (a nasty bird) with the feathers of a dove (a nice bird).

(108-114) Juliet's saying that hearing that Tybalt's dead was upsetting (it "murdered her"), but the word "banished" is 10,000 times worse.

(114-124) She's saying that it'd be sad enough if just Tybalt was dead. Or if there needed to be something else, the Nurse could've said "so's your Mum" or "your dad" or both, after she said Tybalt's dead — that might've led to normal grieving. But the bit that came next, "Romeo is banished", was as bad as saying that Mum, Dad, Tybalt, Romeo and Juliet were dead.

(129) = I'll take you there.

(130-131) = Are they crying over Tybalt's wounds? When they've dried up, I'll be crying over Romeo being banished.

(130-137) Juliet's talking to the rope ladder, saying how it won't be used because Romeo is banished. He made the ladder so he could come to her bed, but now she'll die a virgin-widow.

(137) "maidenhead" = virginity

(138) = Go to your bedroom.

(139) "wot" = know

JULIET O serpent heart, hid with a flowering face!
Did ever dragon keep so fair a cave?
Beautiful tyrant, fiend angelical!   75
Dove-feathered raven, wolvish-ravening lamb!
Despisèd substance of divinest show!
Just opposite to what thou justly seem'st,
A damnèd saint, an honourable villain!
O nature, what hadst thou to do in hell   80
When thou didst bower the spirit of a fiend
In mortal paradise of such sweet flesh?
Was ever book containing such vile matter
So fairly bound? O that deceit should dwell
In such a gorgeous palace!   85

NURSE   There's no trust,
No faith, no honesty in men, all perjured,
All forsworn, all naught, all dissemblers.
Ah, where's my man? Give me some aqua-vitae:
These griefs, these woes, these sorrows make me old.   90
Shame come to Romeo!

JULIET   Blistered be thy tongue
For such a wish! he was not born to shame:
Upon his brow shame is ashamed to sit;
For 'tis a throne where honour may be crowned
Sole monarch of the universal earth.   95
O what a beast was I to chide at him!

NURSE Will you speak well of him that killed your cousin?

JULIET Shall I speak ill of him that is my husband?
Ah, poor my lord, what tongue shall smooth thy name,
When I, thy three-hours wife, have mangled it?   100
But wherefore, villain, didst thou kill my cousin?
That villain cousin would have killed my husband.
Back, foolish tears, back to your native spring,
Your tributary drops belong to woe,
Which you mistaking offer up to joy.   105
My husband lives that Tybalt would have slain,
And Tybalt's dead that would have slain my husband:
All this is comfort, wherefore weep I then?

Some word there was, worser than Tybalt's death,
That murdered me; I would forget it fain,   110
But O, it presses to my memory,
Like damnèd guilty deeds to sinners' minds:
'Tybalt is dead, and Romeo banishèd.'
That 'banishèd', that one word 'banishèd',
Hath slain ten thousand Tybalts. Tybalt's death   115
Was woe enough if it had ended there;
Or if sour woe delights in fellowship,
And needly will be ranked with other griefs,
Why followed not, when she said 'Tybalt's dead',
'Thy father' or 'thy mother', nay, or both,   120
Which modern lamentation might have moved?
But with a rear-ward following Tybalt's death,
'Romeo is banishèd': to speak that word,
Is father, mother, Tybalt, Romeo, Juliet,
All slain, all dead. 'Romeo is banishèd!'   125
There is no end, no limit, measure, bound,
In that word's death, no words can that woe sound.
Where is my father and my mother, Nurse?

NURSE Weeping and wailing over Tybalt's corse.
Will you go to them? I will bring you thither.   130

JULIET Wash they his wounds with tears? mine shall be spent,
When theirs are dry, for Romeo's banishment.
Take up those cords. Poor ropes, you are beguiled,
Both you and I, for Romeo is exiled.
He made you for a highway to my bed,   135
But I, a maid, die maiden-widowèd.
Come, cords, come, Nurse, I'll to my wedding bed,
And death, not Romeo, take my maidenhead!

NURSE Hie to your chamber. I'll find Romeo
To comfort you, I wot well where he is.   140
Hark ye, your Romeo will be here at night.
I'll to him, he is hid at Lawrence' cell.

JULIET O find him! Give this ring to my true knight,
And bid him come to take his last farewell.

Exeunt

(73-79) Juliet's talking about how Romeo's a nice bloke, but he's done a terrible thing. These images are all opposites, for example a raven (a nasty bird) with the feathers of a dove (a nice bird).

(80-82) = what were you up to in hell when you put the spirit of a demon into such a sweet human body?

(83-84) = Has a book containing such horrible stuff ever been in such a nice cover?

(85-87) = You can't trust men.

(88) = Give me some brandy.

(90) = Shame on Romeo!

(90-94) Juliet's telling the Nurse off for being nasty about Romeo, who is far too great to be talked of like that.

(95) "chide" = tell off, be nasty about

(102) = She wants to stop crying.

(105-107) = Romeo is alive, though Tybalt tried to kill him. Tybalt is dead — he tried to kill Romeo. That's comforting, so why am I crying?

Section Nine — The Most Important Scenes

Act 3, Scene 5

Romeo's in Juliet's room, but he has to leave because it's morning. Juliet pretends to her Mum that she's just upset about Tybalt being dead, and that she hates Romeo. Her Dad's arranged for her to marry Paris, but she doesn't want to and they have a big row about it.

(2-3) = It was the nightingale (which sings at night) which you heard, not the lark (which sings in the morning).

(1-7) Juliet doesn't want Romeo to leave, so she tries to tell him it's not morning. But he knows it's morning.

(7-16) Romeo says it must be morning because it's getting lighter, and stars ("night's candles") are gone. He has to leave Verona if he wants to live. But Juliet says the light in the sky is from a meteor, not the sun.

(17-25) Romeo's pretending to agree with her, saying he's happy to stay and die, and that it's not really morning yet.

Oi! That's my singing you're insulting.

(26-28) = It is morning! Go away! It is the lark that's singing badly.

(29-30) This is a pun on 'division', which can mean a load of quickly played notes.

Aargh

(41) She means Romeo should leave through the window.

(46-47) = By this calculation I'll be really old before I see my Romeo again.

(49-50) = I won't miss any chance to send you a message.

(52-53) He's saying that they'll be able to laugh about it all afterwards.

(54) = I have a bad feeling about this.

(60-64) = Fortune chops and changes. Why do you mess with Romeo who is known for his faith? Change then, I hope you'll not keep him long, but send him back to me.

(66-67) = Has she gone to bed really late or got up really early? What unusual reason brings her here?

(69-73) Juliet's Mum misunderstands why Juliet's not well, thinking she's still sad about Tybalt. She tells Juliet that being a bit sad shows you loved him, but being too sad shows you're being silly.

ACT 3 SCENE 5

Juliet's bedroom

Enter ROMEO and JULIET aloft at the window.

JULIET Wilt thou be gone? It is not yet near day:
It was the nightingale, and not the lark,
That pierced the fearful hollow of thine ear;
Nightly she sings on yond pomegranate tree.
Believe me, love, it was the nightingale.

ROMEO It was the lark, the herald of the morn,   5
No nightingale. Look, love, what envious streaks
Do lace the severing clouds in yonder east:
Night's candles are burnt out, and jocund day
Stands tiptoe on the misty mountain tops.
I must be gone and live, or stay and die.   10

JULIET Yond light is not daylight, I know it, I:
It is some meteor that the sun exhaled
To be to thee this night a torch-bearer,
And light thee on thy way to Mantua.
Therefore stay yet, thou need'st not to be gone.   15

ROMEO Let me be tane, let me be put to death,
I am content, so thou wilt have it so.
I'll say yon grey is not the morning's eye,
'Tis but the pale reflex of Cynthia's brow;
Nor that is not the lark whose notes do beat   20
The vanity heaven so high above our heads.
I have more care to stay than will to go:
Come, death, and welcome! Juliet wills it so.
How is't, my soul? Let's talk, it is not day.

JULIET It is, it is, hie hence, be gone, away!   25
It is the lark that sings so out of tune,
Straining harsh discords and unpleasing sharps.
Some say the lark makes sweet division:
This doth not so, for she divideth us.
Some say the lark and loathèd toad changed eyes,   30
O now I would they had changed voices too,
Since arm from arm that voice doth us affray,
Hunting thee hence with hunt's-up to the day.
O now be gone, more light and light it grows.

ROMEO More light and light, more dark and dark our woes!   35

Enter NURSE [hastily].

NURSE Madam!

JULIET Nurse?

NURSE Your lady mother is coming to your chamber.
The day is broke, be wary, look about.   [*Exit*]

JULIET Then, window, let day in, and let life out.

ROMEO Farewell, farewell! One kiss, and I'll descend.
[*He goes down*]

JULIET Art thou gone so, love, lord, ay husband, friend?
I must hear from thee every day in the hour,
For in a minute there are many days.
O, by this count I shall be much in years
Ere I again behold my Romeo!   45

ROMEO [*From below*] Farewell!
I will omit no opportunity
That may convey my greetings, love, to thee.

JULIET O think'st thou we shall ever meet again?   50

ROMEO I doubt it not, and all these woes shall serve
For sweet discourses in our times to come.

JULIET O God, I have an ill-divining soul!
Methinks I see thee now, thou art so low,
As one dead in the bottom of a tomb.   55
Either my eyesight fails, or thou look'st pale.

ROMEO And trust me, love, in my eye so do you:
Dry sorrow drinks our blood. Adieu, adieu!
[*Exit*]

JULIET O Fortune, Fortune, all men call thee fickle;   60
If thou art fickle, what dost thou with him
That is renowned for faith? Be fickle, Fortune:
For then I hope thou wilt not keep him long,
But send him back.

Enter Mother [LADY CAPULET below].

LADY CAPULET Ho, daughter, are you up?   65

JULIET Who is't that calls? It is my lady mother.
Is she not down so late, or up so early?
What unaccustomed cause procures her hither?
[*She goes down from the window and enters below.*]

LADY CAPULET Why how now, Juliet?

JULIET Madam, I am not well.   70

LADY CAPULET Evermore weeping for your cousin's death?
What, wilt thou wash him from his grave with tears?
And if thou couldst, thou couldst not make him live;
Therefore have done. Some grief shows much of love,
But much of grief shows still some want of wit.

JULIET Yet let me weep for such a feeling loss.   75

LADY CAPULET So shall you feel the loss, but not the friend

Left margin notes:

(78-79) = She means that Juliet's not crying because Tybalt's dead, but because his killer, Romeo, is still alive.

(83) = Juliet says that no one hurts her heart as much as Romeo does, but pretends that's because he killed Tybalt.

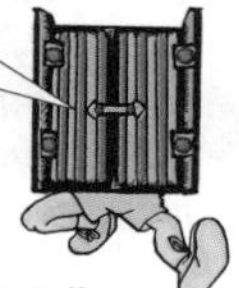

I'm a runnergate

(89) "runagate" = scoundrel (ie Romeo)

(90-91) = give him poison so he'll be dead like Tybalt

(95) "kinsman" = family member

(95) "vexed" = upset

(95) = my poor heart is dead, it mourns for Tybalt so much.

(97) "temper" = mix or change

(103) = You find the means (get the poison) and I'll get someone to do it (give it to Romeo).

(104) = I'll give you some good news.

(106) = What is it may I ask your ladyship?

(107-110) = You have a caring dad who, to cheer you up, has organised a nice surprise that you and I didn't expect.

(112-115) = Next Thursday morning you'll marry Paris at St. Peter's church, and be happy.

Right margin notes:

(118-119) = Why the rush? Why marry before he's even come to court me?

(120) = Mum, please tell Dad

(125) = See how he reacts when you tell him.

(127) = Tybalt

(131) "counterfeits" = resemble

(131 & 133) "bark" = boat

(138) = Have you told our decision? (about marrying Paris)

(139) = Yep, she says 'ta' but she's having none of it.

(141) = Hold on, I'm not with you.

(144) "wrought" = persuaded, organised

(145) He means husband, bridegroom

(148) = although I hate this, I'm grateful because I know you thought I'd like it.

(149) "chopt-logic" = clever twisting of words

(149-153) = Stop mincing words you brat, and get ready for Thursday

(155) "hurdle" = sledge for taking prisoners to be hanged

(157) = Alright, alright, calm down.

(158) = I beg you

Play text:

    Which you weep for.
JULIET   Feeling so the loss,
I cannot choose but ever weep the friend.
LADY CAPULET Well, girl, thou weep'st not so much for his death
    As that the villain lives which slaughtered him. — 80
JULIET What villain, madam?
LADY CAPULET   That same villain Romeo.
JULIET [*Aside*] Villain and he be many miles asunder. -
God pardon him, I do with all my heart:
And yet no man like he doth grieve my heart.
LADY CAPULET That is because the traitor murderer lives.
JULIET Ay, madam, from the reach of these my hands. — 85
Would none but I might venge my cousin's death!
LADY CAPULET We will have vengeance for it, fear thou not:
Then weep no more. I'll send to one in Mantua,
Where that same banished runagate doth live,
Shall give him such an unaccustomed dram — 90
That he shall soon keep Tybalt company;
And then I hope thou wilt be satisfied.
JULIET Indeed I never shall be satisfied
With Romeo, till I behold him - dead -
Is my poor heart, so for a kinsman vexed. — 95
Madam, if you could find out but a man
To bear a poison, I would temper it,
That Romeo should upon receipt thereof
Soon sleep in quiet. O how my heart abhors
To hear him named and cannot come to him, — 100
To wreak the love I bore my cousin
Upon his body that hath slaughtered him!
LADY CAPULET Find thou the means, and I'll find such a man
    But now I'll tell thee joyful tidings, girl.
JULIET And joy comes well in such a needy time. — 105
What are they, beseech your ladyship?
LADY CAPULET Well, well, thou hast a careful father, child,
One who, to put thee from thy heaviness,
Hath sorted out a sudden day of joy,
That thou expects not, nor I looked not for. — 110
JULIET Madam, in happy time, what day is that?
LADY CAPULET Marry, my child, early next Thursday morn,
The gallant, young, and noble gentleman,
The County Paris, at Saint Peter's Church,
Shall happily make thee there a joyful bride. — 115
JULIET Now by Saint Peter's Church and Peter too,
He shall not make me there a joyful bride.

I wonder at this haste, that I must wed
Ere he that should be husband comes to woo.
I pray you tell my lord and father, madam, — 120
I will not marry yet, and when I do, I swear
It shall be Romeo, whom you know I hate,
Rather than Paris. These are news indeed!
LADY CAPULET Here comes your father, tell him so yourself;
And see how he will take it at your hands. — 125

Enter CAPULET and Nurse.

CAPULET When the sun sets, the earth doth drizzle dew,
But for the sunset of my brother's son
It rains downright.
How now, a conduit, girl? What, still in tears?
Evermore showering? In one little body — 130
Thou counterfeits a bark, a sea, a wind:
For still thy eyes, which I may call the sea,
Do ebb and flow with tears; the bark thy body is,
Sailing in this salt flood; the winds, thy sighs,
Who, raging with thy tears and they with them, — 135
Without a sudden calm, will overset
Thy tempest-tossèd body. How now, wife,
Have you delivered to her our decree?
LADY CAPULET Ay, sir; but she will none, she gives you thanks.
I would the fool were married to her grave. — 140
CAPULET Soft, take me with you, take me with you, wife.
How, will she none? Doth she not give us thanks?
Is she not proud? Doth she not count her blest,
Unworthy as she is, that we have wrought
So worthy a gentleman to be her bride? — 145
JULIET Not proud you have, but thankful that you have:
Proud can I never be of what I hate,
But thankful even for hate that is meant love.
CAPULET How how, how how, chopt-logic? What is this?
'Proud', and 'I thank you', and 'I thank you not', — 150
And yet 'not proud', mistress minion you?
Thank me no thankings, nor proud me no prouds,
But fettle your fine joints 'gainst Thursday next,
To go with Paris to Saint Peter's Church,
Or I will drag thee on a hurdle thither. — 155
Out, you green-sickness carrion! Out, you baggage!
You tallow-face!
LADY CAPULET   Fie, fie, what, are you mad?
JULIET Good father, I beseech you on my knees,
Hear me with patience but to speak a word.
    [*She kneels down.*]

CAPULET Hang thee, young baggage, disobedient wretch! 160
I tell thee what: get thee to church a'Thursday,
Or never after look me in the face.
Speak not, reply not, do not answer me!
My fingers itch. Wife, we scarce thought us blest
That God had lent us but this only child, 165
But now I see this one is one too much,
And that we have a curse in having her.
Out on her, hilding!
NURSE   God in heaven bless her!
You are to blame, my lord, to rate her so.
CAPULET And why, my Lady Wisdom? Hold your tongue, 170
Good Prudence, smatter with your gossips, go.
NURSE I speak no treason.
CAPULET   O God-i-goden!
NURSE May not one speak?
CAPULET   Peace, you mumbling fool!
Utter your gravity o'er a gossip's bowl;
For here we need it not.
LADY CAPULET   You are too hot. 175
CAPULET God's bread, it makes me mad! Day, night, work, play,
Alone, in company, still my care hath been
To have her matched; and having now provided
A gentleman of noble parentage,
Of fair demesnes, youthful and nobly ligned, 180
Stuffed, as they say, with honourable parts,
Proportioned as one's thought would wish a man,
And then to have a wretched puling fool,
A whining mammet, in her fortune's tender,
To answer 'I'll not wed, I cannot love; 185
I am too young, I pray you pardon me.'
But and you will not wed, I'll pardon you:
Graze where you will, you shall not house with me.
Look to't, think on't, I do not use to jest.
Thursday is near, lay hand on heart, advise: 190
And you be mine, I'll give you to my friend;
And you be not, hang, beg, starve, die in the streets,
For by my soul, I'll ne'er acknowledge thee,
Nor what is mine shall never do thee good.
Trust to't, bethink you, I'll not be forsworn.   Exit 195
JULIET Is there no pity sitting in the clouds
That sees into the bottom of my grief?
O sweet my mother, cast me not away!
Delay this marriage for a month, a week,
Or if you do not, make the bridal bed 200

In that dim monument where Tybalt lies.
LADY CAPULET Talk not to me, for I'll not speak a word.
Do as thou wilt, for I have done with thee.   Exit
JULIET O God! - O Nurse, how shall this be prevented?
My husband is on earth, my faith in heaven; 205
How shall that faith return again to earth,
Unless that husband send it me from heaven
By leaving earth? Comfort me, counsel me.
Alack, alack, that heaven should practise stratagems
Upon so soft a subject as myself! 210
What say'st thou? Hast thou not a word of joy?
Some comfort, Nurse.
NURSE   Faith, here it is:
Romeo is banished, and all the world to nothing
That he dares ne'er come back to challenge you;
Or if he do, it needs must be by stealth. 215
Then since the case so stands as now it doth,
I think it best you married with the County.
O, he's a lovely gentleman!
Romeo's a dishclout to him. An eagle, madam,
Hath not so green, so quick, so fair an eye 220
As Paris hath. Beshrew my very heart,
I think you are happy in this second match,
For it excels your first, or if it did not,
Your first is dead, or 'twere as good he were
As living here and you no use of him. 225
JULIET Speak'st thou from thy heart?
NURSE And from my soul too, else beshrew them both.
JULIET Amen.
NURSE What?
JULIET Well, thou hast comforted me marvellous much. 230
Go in, and tell my lady I am gone,
Having displeased my father, to Lawrence' cell,
To make confession and to be absolved.
NURSE Marry, I will, and this is wisely done.   [Exit]
JULIET [She looks after Nurse] 235
Ancient damnation! O most wicked fiend!
Is it more sin to wish me thus forsworn,
Or to dispraise my lord with that same tongue
Which she hath praised him with above compare
So many thousand times? Go, counsellor, 240
Thou and my bosom henceforth shall be twain.
I'll to the Friar to know his remedy;
If all else fail, myself have power to die.   Exit

Annotations (lines 164–200):

(164-165) = we thought we were blessed to have this only child

(168) "hilding" = hussy

(169) "rate" = shout at

(171) = go and natter with your cronies

(172) = Goodnight! (get out)

(173-174) = Save your advice for your cronies. We don't need it here.

(176-186) He's saying how annoyed he is that he's spent so much time and effort finding Juliet a really good husband, and now she's whining and making excuses.

(184) = when good fortune's offered her ("mammet" = puppet)

(187-196) = You don't have to get married - you can leave home. Think about it, I don't joke. Thursday's soon, with hand on heart, think about it. If you're my daughter, I'll give you to my friend (Paris). If you're not, then you can hang, beg, starve, or die in the streets, 'cos I promise I'll never recognize you, I'll cut you off from everything that's mine. Believe it. Think about it. I won't change

Annotations (lines 201–242):

(201) She means Tybalt's tomb.

(203) = Do what you want, I'm fed up with you.

(209-210) = Why's heaven picking on poor little me?

(213) = it's a sure thing that

(216) = that's the way things are now

(217) ie Paris

(219-225) = Romeo's a dishcloth compared to him. Paris has got dead nice eyes. Cross my heart, I reckon you'd be happy in this second match, it's better than the first, and if it isn't, your first (Romeo) is dead, or as good as ('cos he's been banished).

(226) = Do you mean it?

(227) = Yep.

(231) = tell Mum

(234) = Indeed I will, it's a good idea.

(235-242) Juliet's really angry at the Nurse for saying bad things about Romeo. The Nurse has always said good things about Romeo before. She says she won't trust the Nurse any more.

(242) = I can kill myself

Section Nine — The Most Important Scenes

ACT 4 SCENE 1
Friar Lawrence's cell

Enter FRIAR LAWRENCE and COUNTY PARIS.
FRIAR LAWRENCE On Thursday, sir? The time is very short.
PARIS My father Capulet will have it so,
And I am nothing slow to slack his haste.
FRIAR LAWRENCE You say you do not know the lady's mind?
Uneven is the course, I like it not. 5
PARIS Immoderately she weeps for Tybalt's death,
And therefore have I little talked of love,
For Venus smiles not in a house of tears.
Now, sir, her father counts it dangerous
That she do give her sorrow so much sway; 10
And in his wisdom hastes our marriage
To stop the inundation of her tears,
Which too much minded by herself alone
May be put from her by society.
Now do you know the reason of this haste. 15
FRIAR LAWRENCE [*Aside*]
I would I knew not why it should be slowed.
Look, sir, here comes the lady toward my cell.
Enter JULIET.
PARIS Happily met, my lady and my wife!
JULIET That may be, sir, when I may be a wife.
PARIS That 'may be' must be, love, on Thursday next. 20
JULIET What must be shall be.
FRIAR LAWRENCE   That's a certain text.
PARIS Come you to make confession to this father?
JULIET To answer that, I should confess to you.
PARIS Do not deny to him that you love me.
JULIET I will confess to you that I love him. 25
PARIS So will ye, I am sure, that you love me.
JULIET If I do so, it will be of more price,
Being spoke behind your back, than to your face.
PARIS Poor soul, thy face is much abused with tears.
JULIET The tears have got small victory by that, 30
For it was bad enough before their spite.
PARIS Thou wrongest it more than tears with that report.
JULIET That is no slander, sir, which is a truth,
And what I spake, I spake it to my face.
PARIS Thy face is mine, and thou hast slandered it. 35
JULIET It may be so, for it is not mine own.
Are you at leisure, holy father, now,
Or shall I come to you at evening mass?

FRIAR LAWRENCE My leisure serves me, pensive daughter, now.
My lord, we must entreat the time alone.
PARIS God shield I should disturb devotion!
Juliet, on Thursday early will I rouse ye;
Till then adieu, and keep this holy kiss. *Exit*
JULIET O shut the door, and when thou hast done so,
Come weep with me, past hope, past cure, past help! 45
FRIAR LAWRENCE O Juliet, I already know thy grief,
It strains me past the compass of my wits.
I hear thou must, and nothing may prorogue it,
On Thursday next be married to this County.
JULIET Tell me not, Friar, that thou hearest of this, 50
Unless thou tell me how I may prevent it.
If in thy wisdom thou canst give no help,
Do thou but call my resolution wise,
And with this knife I'll help it presently.
God joined my heart and Romeo's, thou our hands, 55
And ere this hand, by thee to Romeo's sealed,
Shall be the label to another deed,
Or my true heart with treacherous revolt
Turn to another, this shall slay them both:
Therefore, out of thy long-experienced time, 60
Give me some present counsel, or, behold,
'Twixt my extremes and me this bloody knife
Shall play the umpire, arbitrating that
Which the commission of thy years and art
Could to no issue of true honour bring. 65
Be not so long to speak, I long to die,
If what thou speak'st speak not of remedy.
FRIAR LAWRENCE Hold, daughter, I do spy a kind of hope,
Which craves as desperate an execution
As that is desperate which we would prevent. 70
If, rather than to marry County Paris,
Thou hast the strength of will to slay thyself,
Then is it likely thou wilt undertake
A thing like death to chide away this shame,
That cop'st with Death himself to scape from it; 75
And if thou dar'st, I'll give thee remedy.
JULIET O bid me leap, rather than marry Paris,
From off the battlements of any tower,
Or walk in thievish ways, or bid me lurk
Where serpents are; chain me with roaring bears, 80
Or hide me nightly in a charnel-house,
O'ercovered quite with dead men's rattling bones,

Act 4, Scene 1
Paris, Friar Lawrence and Juliet are talking, then Paris goes, and Juliet says she'd rather kill herself than marry him. Friar Lawrence comes up with the plan to pretend she's dead.

(2) He means father-in-law

(3) = I'm not able to slow him down.

(4-5) Friar L is saying that Paris doesn't know if it's what Juliet wants, and that's not good.

(9-15) Paris explains Lord Capulet wants her to be married, to take her mind off Tybalt's death, and that's the reason for the rush.

(16) Friar L knows the real reason it should be delayed — that Juliet loves Romeo.

(18-36) This is a load of little word games between Paris and Juliet. He calls her his wife, and wants her to admit she loves him, but she just skirts round it.

Thy face is mine.

(37) "at leisure" = free, available

---

(39) = I'm free now.
(40) = we must have privacy
(41) = Heaven forbid that I interrupt religion
(42) = wake you up
(45) She's saying she's beyond hope, or cure, or help.
(47) = I can't bear it
(48) "prorogue" = postpone
(52-54) = If your wisdom can't help me, then call my decision wise, and with this knife I'll help the decision immediately.
(55) (Friar L joined their hands as part of the wedding ceremony.)
(56-59) She's saying that rather than let her hand and her heart be joined to Paris, she will kill herself. Yikes!
(60-67) She's giving Friar L an ultimatum — either he tells her how she can sort things out, or she'll do herself in.
(68-70) = Hold on, I've got an idea, which'll be as dangerous to carry out as what we're trying to avoid is desperate.
(71-75) He's saying she could avoid the shame of marrying Paris, by pretending to be dead.
(77-87) = I'd do all kinds of scary stuff rather than marry Paris.
(81) = A tomb where bones are kept.

Act 4, Scene 2

Juliet comes home and pretends that she's happy to marry Paris now, so Lord Capulet decides to have the wedding a day early.

(1) = *Invite as many guests as I've written down here.*

(3-4) The servant says he'll test which are good cooks by seeing if they'll lick their own fingers.

I can't lick my fingers.

(3 & 6) "ill" = bad

(9) = *We're not ready yet*

(11) = *Yes indeed.*

(13) He's calling Juliet a grumpy, stubborn good-for-nothing.

(14) "shrift" = confession

(15) "gadding" = traipsing about

(16-21) She's saying that talking to Friar Lawrence has shown her that she should do what Lord Capulet says.

(23) Because of what Juliet just said, her dad decides to have the wedding a day early.

(25-26) = *I was as nice as I could be without being too forward.*

(29) = *Yes, indeed*

(30-31) = *Our whole city is much...*

ACT 4 SCENE 2

Capulet's mansion

Enter Father CAPULET, *Mother* [LADY CAPULET], NURSE, *and* SERVINGMEN, *two or three.*

CAPULET So many guests invite as here are writ.

[*Exit Servingman*]

Sirrah, go hire me twenty cunning cooks.

SERVINGMAN You shall have none ill, sir, for I'll try if they can lick their fingers.   5

CAPULET How canst thou try them so?

SERVINGMAN Marry, sir, 'tis an ill cook that cannot lick his own fingers; therefore he that cannot lick his fingers goes not with me.

CAPULET Go, be gone.

[*Exit Servingman*]

We shall be much unfurnished for this time.

What, is my daughter gone to Friar Lawrence?

NURSE Ay forsooth.   10

CAPULET Well, he may chance to do some good on her.

A peevish self-willed harlotry it is.

Enter JULIET.

NURSE See where she comes from shrift with merry look.

CAPULET How now, my headstrong, where have you been gadding?   15

JULIET Where I have learnt me to repent the sin

Of disobedient opposition

To you and your behests, and am enjoined

By holy Lawrence to fall prostrate here

To beg your pardon.

[*She kneels down.*]

Pardon, I beseech you!   20

Henceforward I am ever ruled by you.

CAPULET Send for the County, go tell him of this.

I'll have this knot knit up tomorrow morning.

JULIET I met the youthful lord at Lawrence' cell,

And gave him what becomèd love I might,   25

Not stepping o'er the bounds of modesty.

CAPULET Why, I am glad on't, this is well, stand up.

This is as't should be. Let me see the County;

Ay, marry, go, I say, and fetch him hither.

Now afore God, this reverend holy Friar,   30

All our whole city is much bound to him.

Exeunt

---

(83) smelly limbs

(83) "chapless" = jawless

(88) = *to stay pure to Romeo.*

(89) = *say yes*

(91-118) This is Friar L's plan. She has to go home and pretend to be happy about marrying Paris. Then she goes to bed on her own — the Nurse mustn't be there — and drinks some stuff, which will slow her body down, and make her seem dead for 42 hours. When Paris comes on Thursday morning, he'll think she's dead, and she'll be taken to the family tomb. Meanwhile, Friar L will send Romeo a letter, who will come and take her away to Mantua.

(100) "wanny" = pale

(110) "bier" = funeral bed

(119-120) = *as long as dithering or being scared like a big girl doesn't stop you doing it.*

Don't wuss out.

I won't.

I won't.

(125) = *strength will bring help...*

With reeky shanks and yellow chapless skulls;

Or bid me go into a new-made grave,

And hide me with a dead man in his shroud -   85

Things that to hear them told have made me tremble -

And I will do it without fear or doubt,

To live an unstained wife to my sweet love.

FRIAR LAWRENCE Hold then, go home, be merry, give consent

To marry Paris. Wednesday is tomorrow;   90

Tomorrow night look that thou lie alone,

Let not the Nurse lie with thee in thy chamber.

Take thou this vial, being then in bed,

And this distilling liquor drink thou off,

When presently through all thy veins shall run   95

A cold and drowsy humour; for no pulse

Shall keep his native progress, but surcease;

No warmth, no breath shall testify thou livest;

The roses in thy lips and cheeks shall fade

To wanny ashes, thy eyes' windows fall,   100

Like Death when he shuts up the day of life;

Each part, deprived of supple government,

Shall stiff and stark and cold appear like death,

And in this borrowed likeness of shrunk death

Thou shalt continue two and forty hours,   105

And then awake as from a pleasant sleep.

Now when the bridegroom in the morning comes

To rouse thee from thy bed, there art thou dead.

Then as the manner of our country is,

In thy best robes, uncovered on the bier,   110

Thou shalt be borne to that same ancient vault

Where all the kindred of the Capulets lie.

In the mean time, against thou shalt awake,

Shall Romeo by my letters know our drift,

And hither shall he come, and he and I   115

Will watch thy waking, and that very night

Shall Romeo bear thee hence to Mantua.

And this shall free thee from this present shame,

If no inconstant toy, nor womanish fear,

Abate thy valour in the acting it.   120

JULIET Give me, give me! O tell me not of fear.

FRIAR LAWRENCE Hold, get you gone, be strong and prosperous

In this resolve; I'll send a friar with speed

To Mantua, with my letters to thy lord.

JULIET Love give me strength, and strength shall help afford. 125

Farewell, dear father.

Exeunt

(23) She means if the potion doesn't work then she'll go back to plan A — kill herself with the dagger.

(24-27) = Maybe Friar Lawrence has given me poison to kill me, so that no one will find out he married me to Romeo.

(30-34) = What if I wake up before Romeo comes to save me, won't I suffocate in the airless tomb?

(35) "ere" = "before

(36-54) Juliet's saying how scary it'll be in the tomb, so if she wakes up early it might make her go mad. She talks about it being where her families bones have been put for hundreds of years, where Tybalt is going mouldy, and where there are ghosts. Then she says there'll be horrible smells and noises, and says she might go mad and play with the bones and bash her own brains out.

(55-58) She hallucinates that she can see Tybalt, and then drinks the potion.

Bottoms up!

20
25
30
35
40
45
50
55

My dismal scene I needs must act alone.
Come, vial.
What if this mixture do not work at all?
Shall I be married then tomorrow morning?
No, no, this shall forbid it; lie thou there.
[Laying down her dagger.]
What if it be a poison which the Friar
Subtly hath ministered to have me dead,
Lest in this marriage he should be dishonoured,
Because he married me before to Romeo?
I fear it is, and yet methinks it should not,
For he hath still been tried a holy man.
How if, when I am laid into the tomb,
I wake before the time that Romeo
Come to redeem me? There's a fearful point!
Shall I not then be stifled in the vault,
To whose foul mouth no healthsome air breathes in,
And there die strangled ere my Romeo comes?
Or if I live, is it not very like
The horrible conceit of death and night,
Together with the terror of the place -
As in a vault, an ancient receptacle,
Where for this many hundred years the bones
Of all my buried ancestors are packed,
Where bloody Tybalt, yet but green in earth,
Lies festering in his shroud, where, as they say,
At some hours in the night spirits resort -
Alack, alack, is it not like that I,
So early waking - what with loathsome smells,
And shrieks like mandrakes' torn out of the earth,
That living mortals hearing them run mad -
O, if I wake, shall I not be distraught,
Environèd with all these hideous fears,
And madly play with my forefathers' joints,
And pluck the mangled Tybalt from his shroud,
And in this rage, with some great kinsman's bone,
As with a club, dash out my desp'rate brains?
O look! Methinks I see my cousin's ghost
Seeking out Romeo that did spit his body
Upon a rapier's point. Stay, Tybalt, stay!
Romeo, Romeo, Romeo! Here's drink - I drink to thee.
[She falls upon her bed, within the curtains.]

... to help me sort out the things you think I'll need tomorrow. (She means clothes etc.)

(35-38) Lady Capulet thinks that they shouldn't bring the wedding forward, 'cos they won't have time to prepare. Capulet tells her everything will be fine.

(40) "deck" = dress

(43) = They've all gone out

(45) = for tomorrow

(45-46) = I'm dead happy since Juliet changed her mind.

Act 4, Scene 3
Juliet is alone in her room, getting cold feet about taking the potion ('cos she's scared) but in the end she drinks it.

(1-3) = Yep, those are the best clothes, but I ask you to leave me alone tonight, 'cos I need lots of prayers...

(7-8) = No Mum, we've got all the things ready that we'll need tomorrow.

(14-22) Juliet's feeling scared about what she has to do — taking the potion. For a second she thinks about calling back her mum and the Nurse, then she worries that the potion mightn't work.

JULIET Nurse, will you go with me into my closet,
To help me sort such needful ornaments
As you think fit to furnish me tomorrow?
LADY CAPULET No, not till Thursday, there is time enough. 35
CAPULET Go, Nurse, go with her, we'll to church tomorrow.
                                      Exeunt [Juliet and Nurse]
LADY CAPULET We shall be short in our provision,
'Tis now near night.
CAPULET   Tush, I will stir about,
And all things shall be well, I warrant thee, wife: 40
Go thou to Juliet, help to deck up her;
I'll not to bed tonight; let me alone,
I'll play the housewife for this once. What ho!
They are all forth. Well, I will walk myself
To County Paris, to prepare up him
Against tomorrow. My heart is wondrous light, 45
Since this same wayward girl is so reclaimed.
                                                        Exeunt

ACT 4 SCENE 3
Juliet's bedroom
Enter JULIET and NURSE.
JULIET Ay, those attires are best, but, gentle Nurse,
I pray thee leave me to myself tonight:
For I have need of many orisons
To move the heavens to smile upon my state,
Which, well thou knowest, is cross and full of sin. 5
Enter Mother[LADY CAPULET].
LADY CAPULET What, are you busy, ho? Need you my help?
JULIET No, madam, we have culled such necessaries
As are behoveful for our state tomorrow.
So please you, let me now be left alone,
And let the Nurse this night sit up with you, 10
For I am sure you have your hands full all,
In this so sudden business.
LADY CAPULET   Good night.
Get thee to bed and rest, for thou hast need.
                              Exeunt[Lady Capulet and Nurse]
JULIET Farewell! God knows when we shall meet again. 15
I have a faint cold fear thrills through my veins
That almost freezes up the heat of life:
I'll call them back again to comfort me.
Nurse! - What should she do here?

ACT 4 SCENE 4

A room in Capulet's mansion
Enter lady of the house LADY CAPULET and NURSE with herbs.
LADY CAPULET Hold, take these keys and fetch more spices, Nurse.
NURSE They call for dates and quinces in the pastry.
Enter old CAPULET.
CAPULET Come, stir, stir, stir! The second cock hath crowed,
The curfew bell hath rung, 'tis three a'clock.
Look to the baked meats, good Angelica,
Spare not for cost.   5
NURSE   Go, you cot-quean, go,
Get you to bed. Faith, you'll be sick tomorrow
For this night's watching.
CAPULET No, not a whit. What, I have watched ere now
All night for lesser cause, and ne'er been sick.   10
LADY CAPULET Ay, you have been a mouse-hunt in your time,
But I will watch you from such watching now.
Exeunt Lady [Capulet] and Nurse
CAPULET A jealous hood, a jealous hood!
*Enter three or four [SERVINGMEN]
with spits and logs and baskets.*
                                   Now, fellow,
What is there?
FIRST SERVINGMAN Things for the cook, sir, but I know not what. 15
CAPULET Make haste, make haste.
                                      [*Exit First Servingman*]
                                 Sirrah, fetch drier logs.
SECOND SERVINGMAN I have a head, sir, that will find out logs,
And never trouble Peter for the matter.
CAPULET Mass, and well said, a merry whoreson, ha!   20
Thou shalt be loggerhead.
                    [*Exeunt Second Servingman and any others*]
                               Good faith, 'tis day.
The County will be here with music straight,
For so he said he would.
Play music [within].
                          I hear him near.
Nurse! Wife! What ho! What, Nurse, I say!
Enter Nurse.
Go waken Juliet, go and trim her up,   25
I'll go and chat with Paris. Hie, make haste,
Make haste, the bridegroom he is come already,
Make haste, I say.
                                                         [*Exit*]

Act 4, Scene 4
Lord Capulet is organising the celebrations for the wedding between Juliet and Paris.

(3-6) = Hurry up! It's late! Make sure there are enough baked meats Angelica, don't worry about the cost.

(6-7) = Go to bed you house-husband. You'll be ill tomorrow for lack of sleep.

(9-10) = Nah, I've stayed up all night before — when I didn't have such a good reason — and wasn't ill.

(11) = When you were younger, you stayed up late hunting women. I'll make sure you go to bed now.

No — fetch drier logs.

(18-19) = I can find the logs without bothering Peter.

(20-21) Lord Capulet making a joke of what the servant said of logs and his head, calling him a "loggerhead" (a blockhead).

(23-24) = Blimey, it's daytime. Paris will be here soon (straight away) with the musicians

(25) = make her look ace

(27) "make haste"

EEEEK! He's here already. Go and tart my daughter up.

Little do they know...

Index

A

A plague a'both your houses 96
a rose/By any other word would smell as sweet 92
Act 1 Scene 1 44
Act 1 Scene 2 45
Act 1 Scene 3 45
Act 1 Scene 4 46
Act 1 Scene 5 46, 90
Act 2 Scene 1 47
Act 2 Scene 2 47, 92
Act 2 Scene 3 48
Act 2 Scene 4 48
Act 2 Scene 5 49
Act 2 Scene 6 49
Act 3 Scene 1 50, 95
Act 3 Scene 2 51, 98
Act 3 Scene 3 51
Act 3 Scene 4 52
Act 3 Scene 5 52, 100
Act 4 Scene 1 53, 103
Act 4 Scene 2 53, 104
Act 4 Scene 3 53, 105
Act 4 Scene 4 54, 106
Act 4 Scene 5 54
Act 5 Scene 1 55
Act 5 Scene 2 55
Act 5 Scene 3 56
action 68
actors 10, 13
advice for the lovers 41
ambitious mum 39
anon 91, 93
answer in order 73
answering the writing task 7, 60, 61, 64, 65, 82, 83, 84, 86, 87
answering - endings 66
answering - the start 63
answering the question 74
arranged marriage 18
atmosphere 78
audience 13, 87, 78
authority 23

B

back up what you're saying 13
background knowledge 85
balcony scene 92
beginnings 73

B (continued)

Benvolio 33, 37
beseech 94,101
blank verse 26
bloodthirsty woman 39

C

Capulets 2, 15, 16, 17, 33, 35, 39
cat's 48
character writing task 5, 7, 9, 68
characters 1, 8, 13, 14, 16, 33, 58, 79
chorus 14, 47
church 20
church law 52
common images 29
comparisons 84
confidential advice 20
costumes 10
Count Paris 33
County 42
cowards 16
coz 90
customs 1

D

dark 29
death 1, 13, 17
defending Romeo 17
differences writing task 4
director 10
divide your time 83
double meanings 31
duels 16

E

egging Tybalt on 80
ending 73
ending your answer 66
enter 14
epic similes 28
ere 105
essay plan 69
examiners' tips 63, 70, 82, 83, 84, 86, 87
examples 10
excitement 78, 79, 82, 84, 86
execute Romeo or not 79
exeunt 14

E (continued)

exit 14
explaining your quote 86

F

family 18
fancy fencing term 81
fate 30
feud 15, 17, 19, 38, 44, 47
fights 16, 17, 44, 80, 95
finishing your answer 76, 87
first paragraph 74
flowers 30
following your plan 83
Friar Lawrence 20, 33, 41

G

good marks 8, 9
grammar 76

H

handy hints 78, 84
herbaceous dude 48
hints for a plan 82
honour 15, 16, 17, 19
"how does Shakepeare...." writing tasks 5

I

images in the play 28, 29, 30
insulting Tybalt 81
interesting words 10
introductions 14, 63

J

jokes 31
Juliet writing question 58
Juliet's character 19, 33, 35, 59, 61
Juliet drinks the potion 105
Juliet's problems 64

K

key points 60
King of Cats 81
kinsman 101

L

language use 9, 22, 26, 28, 79
lark 100
lest 93
light 29
link up your points 64, 84
long sentences 25

Index

looking at the scene 79
Lord & Lady Capulet 33, 39
Lord & Lady Montague 33, 38
love 1, 2, 12, 15, 19, 28, 35
love scene 23

M
main events of the play 2
mammet 1002
marriage 18, 19, 20, 33
marry 102
Mercutio 17, 33, 36
Mercutio vs. Tybalt 95
metaphor 28
method for answering tasks 59
middle 73
Montague 17, 34, 38
Montagues 2, 15, 16, 17, 33,
          34, 38
mood tasks 9, 13, 78, 80

N
nephew 37
new paragraph 73
nightingale 100
nitty-gritty for answers 63
notes 7, 62, 71, 72
Nurse 33, 40

O
old windbag 40
old words 27
on stage 80, 84
opinions 9

P
paragraphs 10, 74, 86
paragraph finish 87
Paris 42
party 45, 90
personification 28
planning your answer
      62, 82, 83
poetry 1, 22, 23, 24, 25, 26
points to help writing 64, 65,
      83, 86
points to end 66
potion — Juliet drinks it 105
Prince 42
Prince of Cats 36

professional dead tree 14
prologue 14, 26, 44
prorogue 103
prose 22, 23
proving your points 86
punctuation 10, 25, 76
puns 31

Q
questions with two parts 58
quoting 65, 74, 80, 86

R
read the scene 70
reading in detail 80, 81
reading in the exam 6, 62
reading poetry 24, 25
reading tasks 69
religion 20
revision summary 11, 21, 32,
          43, 58, 77, 88
Reynard the Fox 36
rhyme 26
Romeo's character 17, 33,
          34, 44, 82
Romeo vs. Tybalt 95
rough notes 82

S
sacred 20
sanctuary 20
scenes — important ones 90
sea images 29
secret wedding 2
self-respect 17
setting of the play 15, 85
shorthand 82
silly blunders 76
similarities writing task 4
similes 28
sirrah 90
skim read 79
sonnets 26
spelling 10, 76
stage directions 14, 58, 79
stars 30
stick to the plan 83
stories 9
summing up the scene 87
sword fighting 13, 44, 50, 95

syllables 26
syllables in poetry 24

T
taking the mickey 36
tasks SAT style 4, 5, 7, 58, 63,
          86, 69, 78, 84, 86
tense and exciting bits 78
tension 78, 79, 80, 82, 84, 86
The Prince 33
thee 27
things get worse 19
thou 27
thy 27
till death do us part 56
time for your ending 87
tough cookies 35
tragedy 14
tricky play words 14
trust 20
Tybalt 16, 17, 33, 37, 44
Tybalt vs. Mercutio 95
Tybalt vs. Romeo 95

U
understanding the scene 8
using the whole play 85

V
Verona 1, 2, 3, 15, 16, 19
verse 26
versions of the play 10

W
watch 56
way people say things 79
wedding stuff 41, 45
what happens in the play 2, 3
what happens in the scene 79
what light through yonder window breaks
      92
wherefore art though Romeo 92
wordplay 36
writing a clear answer 84
writing about characters 58
writing as a character 68
writing the answer 64, 65
writing well 10

Y
yond 91